Attic, Basement and Garage Conversion

A Do-It-Yourselfer's Guide

For Rose

For your patience, for your support, for being you.
Always know that however busy I am,
no sentence I write
could ever mean as much to me as you do.

Attic, Basement and Garage Conversion
A Do-It-Yourselfer's Guide

Paul Bianchina

TAB BOOKS Inc.
Blue Ridge Summit, PA

FIRST EDITION
FIRST PRINTING

Library of Congress Cataloging-in-Publication Data

Bianchina, Paul.
　　Attic, basement, and garage conversion : a do-it-yourselfer's
guide / by Paul Bianchina.
　　　　p.　　　cm.
　　ISBN 0-8306-9271-1　　　ISBN 0-8306-3271-9 (pbk.)
　　1. Attics—Remodeling—Amateurs' manuals.　2. Basements-
-Remodeling—Amateurs' manuals.　3. Garages—Remodeling—Amateurs'
manuals. I. Title.

TH4816.3.A77B52　1989　　　　　　　　　　　　89-39630
643'.5—dc20　　　　　　　　　　　　　　　　　　CIP

TAB BOOKS Inc. offers software for sale. For information and a catalog, please contact TAB Software Department, Blue Ridge Summit, PA 17294-0850.

Questions regarding the content of this book should be addressed to:

Reader Inquiry Branch
TAB BOOKS Inc.
Blue Ridge Summit, PA 17294-0214

Acquisitions Editor: Kimberly Tabor
Book Editor: Kathleen E. Beiswenger
Production: Katherine Brown
Cover Design: Lorie E. Schlosser
Cover photographs courtesy of Georgia Pacific.

Contents

Acknowledgments

I would like to express my deep appreciation to the following individuals and companies for their assistance in the preparation of this book. In particular, I would like to thank Rose for her quiet patience throughout this long process; Mike O'Brien and staff at Western Wood Products Association for the long hours spent combing their slide files; Barbara Eden for the use of all her files; Ann Madden at Velux-America Incorporated for all her photographs; Myra Collum at Georgia-Pacific Corporation for the volume of material she sent; Kim Tabor at TAB BOOKS Inc. for her undying patience; and Steve Manina for putting up with me and my camera. I would also like to thank:

American Plywood Association
American Home Lighting Institute
American Standard
Andersen Windows
Celotex Corporation
Dow Chemical Company
Georgia-Pacific Corporation
Kohler Company
Louisiana-Pacific Corporation
Manina Construction
NuTone Products
Spectrum Construction

x □ *Acknowledgments*

Velux-America Corporation
Webb Manufacturing Incorporated
Western Wood Products Association
Wilsonart
Wood Moulding and Millwork Producers Association

Introduction

In virtually all of today's homes attics, basements, and garages represent major unused or underused areas. The potential for developing these areas into usable living space is tremendous. The spaces are already enclosed and weathertight, and in many cases they require only imagination and a little finish work to convert them into new, attractive rooms.

Attic, basement, and garage conversions can gain badly needed space in a home at a fraction of the cost of a complete room addition. The roof is already in place, as are the exterior walls and all or part of the floor. What more could a remodeler ask?

The possibilities are endless: new bedrooms or bathrooms for a growing family; a complete shop for the handyman or the hobbyist; a well-appointed work space and studio for a comfortable home office; or perhaps a lavish new game room, complete with antique pool table, oak wet bar, and the latest in video games.

In homes sorely lacking extra storage space, these areas can be a treasure trove of nooks and crannies for storing a lifetime of accumulated items. Back under the eaves, beneath the stairway, and along entire walls, storage spaces and opportunities abound. With some careful planning and some basic tools, almost anything can be achieved in a surprisingly short amount of time.

Perhaps best of all, attics, basements, and garages are perfectly suited for remodeling by the do-it-yourselfer. Many projects require only basic carpentry skills, with little complicated cutting or heavy structural work. And because the rooms are already enclosed, they can be redone a little at a time with no weather or security worries, and no time constraints. Summer or winter, converting these dusty spaces into welcome additions to the house can be fun, inexpensive, and a real source of pride, enjoyment, and increased value.

If you're thinking of remodeling your attic, basement, or garage, you're holding the one book that tells you everything you need to know: the tools and techniques for planning and design, carpentry and framing, windows and skylights, floors and floor coverings, storage, finish work and trim—all in one clear, easily understood volume.

Attic, Basement and Garage Conversion: A Do-It-Yourselfer's Guide, combined with your skills and imagination, can open up a whole new vista of exciting living space that's hiding under your roof right now!

1
Uses and Planning

FOR MANY PEOPLE, THE PLANNING STAGES OF A NEW REMODELING PROJECT ARE among the most enjoyable (FIG. 1-1). Ideas flow, notepads are crammed with sketches and possibilities, and excitement grows as the project moves toward reality. Creating a new living space in your home—defining an area for new and perhaps long-awaited family activities—is truly exciting.

Thorough and well-thought-out plans are crucial for a successful remodeling project that serves your needs and meets your expectations. So sit back, pick up your pencil and notebook, and plan on spending a few enjoyable evenings planning your new space.

WHAT DO YOU HOPE
TO GAIN FROM YOUR REMODELING?

Perhaps the first question you should ask yourself is what you hope to achieve with the remodeling. What is it you really need? Are you hoping for a home office? A family room? An extra bathroom? Do you need to expand your home's storage space or create room for overnight guests?

These questions, although they might seem obvious to you if you've been thinking about this project for a long time, need to be reconsidered and explored in some depth. Remodeling to create areas that don't serve your needs is little better than not remodeling at all, and it often can be an expensive and frustrating experience. Time spent answering a few questions now will help you tremendously at every subsequent stage of the project.

(COURTESY OF AMERICAN PLYWOOD ASSOCIATION)

Fig. 1-1. A beautifully renovated attic can add living space and value to any home.

What will the room(s) be used for? Be very specific in answering this question because this is where you will really begin to define your needs and requirements. For example, if your answer is "family room," what activities do you hope to provide for? Which family members will use the room? Will it be for family only, for occasional guests, or for frequent entertaining?

If the new room is to be an office, how many people will it serve? Will it be for home use only, or will you be conducting an actual business from that room? Will clients or customers ever visit you there?

In the case of a hobby room or studio, what activities will take place there? Will you need to provide additional amounts of natural light for painting or sculpting? How many people would want to use the room, and how many different hobbies or crafts will need to be accommodated?

What special equipment or amenities will be needed? This is another very important consideration. All too often, people will seek to set up a room for a specific use, without thinking through completely what that room will require to be fully functional. Once again, consider some examples.

For the family room, do you wish to install a pool table or Ping-Pong area? Will there be a television, and if so, will antenna or cable provisions need to be made? Do you wish to provide a wet bar or perhaps even a small refrigerator or microwave? Will areas be set aside for music, reading, darts, video games, or other specific activities? What furniture do you wish to have in the room, and how many people do you wish to accommodate?

How many desks will your office need? Will there be file cabinets or perhaps a drafting table? Will you need to provide for a computer, printer, copy machine, typewriter, or other office furniture? What about telephone lines, either as an extension or as a separate line? Will any of the equipment you're using require special electrical circuits? Also, if the office will be used by clients who are visiting you, can you separate the office from your normal living areas, and can you provide a separate entrance into the office from outside? (See FIG. 1-2.)

(COURTESY OF AMERICAN PLYWOOD ASSOCIATION)

Fig. 1-2. A two-car garage such as this one can be converted easily to living space—the walls, floor, and roof are already finished.

Will your hobby room need any special equipment in it? What about additional ventilation for paint fumes or odors from other hobby activities? Do you wish to install a dark room, or will any other activities in the room require plumbing facilities? How about worktables, counter space, and storage?

Perhaps your new room will be a bedroom or bathroom, or even both. What furniture will you need in the room? How many people will occupy it? Will the bathroom be just big enough for a toilet and sink, or do you want to install a shower or a bathtub? If the bathroom or bedroom is being set up for an ill or elderly person, what special access, fixtures, or other unusual needs will have to be considered?

What are your specific storage needs? This is something else to plan. Will you be storing a lot of office supplies or hobby materials? How about games, books, records, or other items for the family room? How much closet space will the bathroom require? How about extra linen, blankets, or even medical supplies?

YOUR WISH LIST

A very helpful way of focusing your plans and ideas, prioritizing your needs, and keeping your budget realistic is to make up a wish list. On the list, make a note of anything and everything you can think of that you want your remodeling project to include. Don't think that something is too small or too silly to be included—if it's at all important to you, put it on the list. If other family members will be using the room, it's important to get their input too.

Now, go back down the list and prioritize each item. Write "1" in front of an item if it's something you simply must have; write "2" if it's an item you'd like to have if possible; and write "3" if it's something you'd like but could live without. For instance, if the whole reason for the new family room is to put a pool table in it, then the pool table is an obvious "1."

Now go back over the list a second time and see if you want to change any numbers. Most people's budgets will require dropping all of the "3" items right away. Some of the "2's" will survive a little longer. The trick is to keep all the "1's"—the priority items. This simple process will go a long way toward getting you the rooms you want at a price you can afford.

ZONING RESTRICTIONS

Before getting too far along, you should check and see if any of your remodeling plans violate local zoning or planning commission restrictions. For example, some areas might not allow you to operate a business from your home if that business requires storing equipment or materials, operating certain types of equipment, or having clients visit you on a regular basis. (Check with your insurance agent also for specific business liability and business equipment insurance. These items might not be covered under your normal homeowner's insurance.)

Another possible problem might be encountered if you wish to remodel an attic, basement, or garage to convert it into an apartment for rent. In general terms, you will need to provide at least 400 square feet of living area, with kitchen and bathroom facilities. Your home must be located in an area that is zoned for apartment use, and you will also need to meet access, fire, and emergency egress (exit) requirements.

Before undertaking a remodeling for the purposes of creating a commercial office or an apartment, or if you have any questions about the intended scope or use of your remodeling project, consult your local planning department. Also, don't overlook the possible need for a business license or other special licenses and permits.

SPECIFIC ROOM REQUIREMENTS

The following guide to some of the more common attic, garage, or basement rooms might be helpful in evaluating what you need. In most cases, the guide lists minimum recommended sizes and areas, or minimum building code requirements. Wherever possible, allowing additional space above these minimums will increase the practicality of the room and your enjoyment of it.

Also listed here are some suggestions for counters, storage facilities, and other items your room will probably need. Add these suggestions to the lists of specific needs you outlined above to help you define exactly what you'd like your room to contain.

Family Room

In homes cramped for living space, especially for families with older children or teenagers, the family room is the perennial favorite remodeling project (FIG. 1-3). It provides a combination game center, entertaining area,

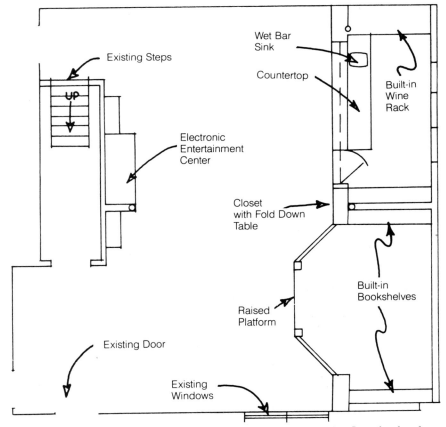

Fig. 1-3. A good remodeling project requires careful preplanning. Here is a floor plan for a basement renovation, including all the major features. (COURTESY OF GEORGIA-PACIFIC CORPORATION)

and central meeting place, and often quickly becomes the most-used room in the house. For your family room, try to provide:

□ A fairly spacious area, preferably at least 14 × 16 feet. If the room will accommodate a pool table, remember to provide a minimum of 4 feet (preferably 5 feet) around the table on all sides to allow for using the cue sticks.

□ Good natural and artificial lighting. You might wish to split the lighting into task groups, providing specific lights for television areas, game areas, hobby areas, etc.

□ Plenty of electrical outlets, along with special wiring for television, stereo (FIG 1-4), and computer as needed. And don't forget the telephone!

□ Space for seating, game playing, and informal entertaining. Make this area, 8 to 10 feet square, if possible, to allow for furniture and comfortable spacing.

□ Convenient access to a bathroom (FIG. 1-5) and to the kitchen. If the kitchen is a long distance away, try to provide an area for snack storage and consider adding a small refrigerator, microwave, and coffee pot. (Consider these items as well when doing your electrical wiring.)

□ Ample storage, including areas for games, records, and books. Provide specific shelving units or other storage areas for stereo and television equipment.

□ An outside exit, if possible. This allows for outside entertaining and emergency exits, and takes some strain off the home's regular traffic patterns.

Fig. 1-4. Basements abound with nooks and crannies that, when properly finished and wired, provide a space for all sorts of objects.

(COURTESY OF VELUX-AMERICA INC.)

Fig. 1-5. This attic master bathroom has fixed and operable roof windows for maximum light and ventilation.

Bedroom

The bedroom is another favorite remodeling project. For a growing family or to accommodate out-of-town guests, converting unused space into a bedroom really can improve an overcrowded home (FIG. 1-6).

Of primary importance with a bedroom is being able to meet the building code requirements for emergency exit, known as *egress*. The Uniform Building Code requires either an exterior door or a window with an operable area of not less than 5.7 square feet. In addition, the window must have a minimum clear opening width of 20 inches and a minimum clear opening height of 24 inches. The sill must not be more than 44 inches above the floor.

A bedroom also needs adequate light and ventilation, which usually is provided through operable doors, windows, or skylights. The glass area for light must equal a minimum of one-tenth of the room's floor area, and the ventilation openings (doors or the operable portion of a window or skylight) must equal a minimum of one-twentieth of the room's floor area.

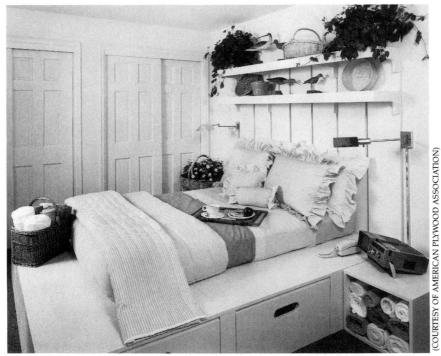

(COURTESY OF AMERICAN PLYWOOD ASSOCIATION)

Fig. 1-6. A basement or garage remodel offers ample space for a spare bedroom such as this one.

The building code minimum for a bedroom used by one person is 70 square feet, with no horizontal room dimension of less than 7 feet. Provide an area of 140 to 160 square feet for a master bedroom. Some generally accepted space minimums for bedrooms are 18 to 22 inches on each side of the bed for making it up; 45 inches at the foot of the bed or along one side for dressing; and 5 feet of closet space per person, with a minimum depth of 24 inches.

Other factors to consider when designing a bedroom include:

□ Smoke detector. Mount it on the wall or within 12 inches of the ceiling, at the top of the attic stairs, or in the basement. It must be audible to all sleeping areas.
□ Convenient access to a bathroom. Consider creating a new half bathroom as part of the new bedroom area (FIG. 1-7).
□ Positioning windows. If possible, try to position bedroom windows for east exposure (morning light) or south exposure (cheerful, warm light in the winter). Avoid west-facing windows, especially in the attic, as they contribute to heat buildup in the summer.
□ Ample electrical outlets, stereo and television cables, and a telephone.

(COURTESY OF AMERICAN STANDARD)

Fig. 1-7. Part of this large, open-beam attic was converted into a spacious bathroom for two.

Home Office

With the growing number of home businesses, and the equally large number of homes linked by computer to their office, the home office has become a remodeling priority for many people. Even if you don't have a business at home, creating a space where you can take care of the daily running of your household can be a surprisingly convenient and pleasant area to get away from everything.

Attics and basements are especially well suited for use as offices. They are away from the normal daily activities of the home, both from a physical and noise standpoint. Plus, ascending or descending the stairs to get to your office gives you privacy and a "leaving home" feeling that stimulates your productivity. Some of the more important design considerations for your home office include:

□ High levels of natural and artificial light, particularly at desk, computer, and drawing areas.
□ Sound insulation in the walls, in the floor (for an attic office), or in the ceiling (for a basement office). You should also consider a good-quality, solid-core door to close the office off from the stairway and to minimize noise reflected along the stairs from the living areas of the house.
□ Special circuits for computer equipment and copiers, along with ample electrical and telephone outlets. (You might want to skip a television cable in this room!).
□ Ample room for file storage—both active and dead files—along with shelving for books, manuals, and other reference materials. Provide ample room for storing office supplies, also.

Remember that to accommodate a small desk, desk chair, typing table, and file cabinet, you will need a room at least 8 feet × 8 feet. If you need to accommodate other equipment, or if you want to allow for future expansion, be sure to plan accordingly. You'll also want to remember that you need a minimum of 36 inches of clear area in front of a bookcase and 42 inches in front of a file cabinet.

Special-Use Room

Other possible uses for your remodeled space might be a sewing room, music room, studio, library, hobby room, workshop, or laundry area (FIG. 1-8). For all of these types of rooms, provide lots of natural light, either from windows, skylights, or a combination of both.

Sewing Room. You'll need a table for the sewing machine. This table should be desk height—(29 to 31 inches off the floor)— and have 18 to 36 inches of counter space on both sides of the machine. Also, you'll want to provide a worktable for cutting patterns—36 to 42 inches high, according to your preference, and a minimum of 36 inches wide. Finally, allow ample storage for material, thread, sewing implements, and other items you'll want to keep close at hand.

Music Room, Studio, and Library. These rooms thrive on privacy and quiet. Provide sound insulation in the walls, floor, and ceiling (FIG. 1-9), and lots of good lighting. Also, allow ample bookshelf area for the library, along with space for at least two comfortable chairs and a table.

Hobby Room. Depending on the specific needs of the hobby, this room can vary greatly. If the room is large enough to accommodate several different hobby activities, you can usually combine storage and counter space to

(COURTESY OF NUTONE, INC.)

Fig. 1-8. A built-in ironing board offers tremendous convenience, especially in a small laundry area.

maximize the use of available space. Allow good lighting, particularly at the work areas; good ventilation, including an exhaust fan capable of five to six air changes per hour; plenty of electrical outlets grouped along the work counters; ample closed storage to keep the room looking neat and organized while keeping potentially dangerous hobby supplies and tools away from children; and, if possible, provide a sink with hot and cold water.

(COURTESY OF ARMSTRONG)

Fig. 1-9. Glass block and acoustic ceiling tiles help make this garage conversion into a well-appointed office/study/library.

Workshop. If you're converting a basement or garage into a woodworking or metalworking shop, your needs will vary again with the tools you have (or expect to acquire) and the activities taking place in the shop. In general, you'll need ample floor space for safe access to the tools; worktables or benches, which can be caster-mounted to roll aside when not needed; and specialized storage areas for the materials you'll be using. Also pay careful attention to the access you have into these areas—it can be very frustrating trying to maneuver a full sheet of plywood through the kitchen and down the basement steps to the shop.

Laundry. A laundry area requires a minimum of approximately 60 inches in width and 36 inches in depth to accommodate a standard washer and dryer. If possible, allow additional space for a folding counter, a laundry sink, and temporary storage for clean and soiled clothes. The laundry area, in addition to its plumbing requirements, also requires a dedicated 120-volt, 20-amp laundry circuit (only one outlet on it) for the washer, and a 240-volt, 30-amp circuit for the electric dryer.

LIGHTING

Not to be overlooked in the planning stages of your remodeling project is the need for good lighting. Providing the proper levels of light in each room increases your comfort and safety and, at the same time, enhances the room's appearance and decor.

Lighting is not something to take for granted by simply placing a fixture in the middle of the ceiling or a few table lamps around the room. Here are some specific guidelines from the American Home Lighting Institute:

Reading. 75- to 100-watt (W) incandescent bulbs or 32W to 22/32W fluorescent. Place shades, whether on portable lamps or pendants, at eye level: about 40 to 42 inches above the floor.

Game Tables. Use a recessed 150W incandescent or two 40W fluorescents over each half of a Ping-Pong table. For a pool table, use a 100W shaded incandescent or a 150W "R" flood over each half of the table. Use a 100W pendant over a game table. Place hanging fixtures over game tables approximately 36 inches above the tabletop.

Television and Computer. Provide a low level of general lighting that does not wash out the screen.

Pianos and Music Stands. Use recessed eyeball fixture or track light equipped with a minimum 75W "R" or "PAR" flood bulb. Place it 12 inches to the left and 24 inches behind the music. (Two fixtures, 30 inches apart, and aimed at the music is even better.) Properly positioned portable lamps can also be used.

Desk Area. For hanging or desk lamps, use 150W to 225W incandescent or 32W to 22/32W fluorescent, with the shade approximately 15 inches above the work surface. Fluorescent wall brackets are also good when used with a 30W or 40W tube positioned 15 to 18 inches above the surface of the desk.

Sewing. For sewing (FIG. 1-10), provide approximately twice as much light as allowed for reading. Position the light 12 inches to the left and 6 inches behind the individual work areas and aim it at the work.

Bathroom Mirror. For small mirrors, place two 75W to 120W incandescent lights about 30 inches apart on each side of the mirror, centered 60 inches above the floor, in addition to a 100W to 120W ceiling fixture. For mirrors over 36 inches wide, use an incandescent strip at least 22 inches long over the top of the mirror, with three or four 60W bulbs.

Stairs. Provide a light at the top and bottom of the stairs, separately switched for convenience. Provide an additional light at landings.

Laundry. For an average-sized room of 75 to 120 square feet, provide one to four incandescent bulbs totaling 150W to 200W, or a 60W to 80W fluorescent.

Workshop. Provide a minimum of 2 watts of incandescent light per square foot, or 3/4 watt of fluorescent light per square foot. Suspend additional fluorescent work lights over workbenches, approximately 48 inches above the bench surface.

Fig. 1-10. An example of proper lighting in the laundry and sewing room.

(COURTESY OF AMERICAN HOME LIGHTING INSTITUTE)

PLANS AND PERMITS

Your remodeling project will require a set of plans detailing the appearance and specifications of the work you want to do, plus building permits that cover any structural, electrical, plumbing, or heating and air-conditioning work you'll be doing. The building inspectors will review your plans to check for proper sizes, clearances, building materials, structural details, and other aspects of the work, then they will issue a building permit. They will make periodic visits to the job site, at your request, as each phase of the work is completed. This is to ensure proper compliance with the building codes and guarantee the safety of the finished project.

The types of plans you'll need to submit and the number of details they contain varies between different locations and projects, so check with the building department for specific details before beginning your drawings. For a typical attic, basement, or garage remodeling, you will need to prepare and submit the following plans.

Floor Plan. This shows the finished room as if you were looking straight down on it. The floor plan details where the walls, windows, and doors will go as well as the location of plumbing fixtures, cabinets, and other features of the job. Structural details, such as the size of the floor joists and roof rafters, are also called out on the floor plan.

Elevations. If you will be making changes to the exterior appearance of the house, you will also need to submit elevations. These drawings show the appearance of the outside of the house as you look straight in at each wall. They include such details as the window and door location and type, the type of siding and roofing material you'll be using, and the pitch of the roof.

Plot Plan. This drawing simply shows the size of your lot or acreage and the position of the house on the property. Also shown are the main road in front of your house; sidewalks and driveways; detached buildings such as garages, storage sheds, or barns; and large trees, streams, or other details of the property. This drawing is dimensioned to show how far the house sits back from each of the property lines.

DOING IT YOURSELF

Another big question at this point in the planning is whether you wish to do any or all of the work yourself. Taking on a home remodeling project of this scope offers some obvious rewards—and some perhaps not-so-obvious drawbacks.

Doing the work yourself allows you to maintain total control over the project, from the selection of all the materials to installation of the final nail. You're spared the hassle of contacting a contractor and going through the bidding process. Without regular payment schedules to meet, you have more freedom over your budgeting. And finally, you have the two items that appeal to do-it-yourselfers the most—the opportunity to save some of the construction costs (although exactly how much you'll save is difficult to determine, especially if you place a monetary value on your time) and the pride associated with having done the work yourself.

On the other side of the coin are perhaps the biggest do-it-yourself draw-backs—time and inconvenience. If you're already working full time, facing a major remodeling project that eats up most of your nights and weekends might cause the work to lose its appeal quickly. Also, you face the inconvenience of a much longer completion time—there's no contractor at your house doing the work during the day while you're away.

You will be faced with having to order materials and either pick them up or arrange for their delivery. You'll have to schedule any subcontractors you're using (the plumber, the electrician, etc.) and be certain the work is at a point where you're ready for them.

Before making the decision to undertake the entire project yourself, take a moment for a little honest self-appraisal. How much time do you have to give to the project? How soon do you need it completed? Do you have the expertise to complete all the various aspects of the project? Do you have, or are you willing to buy or rent, the necessary tools you'll need?

For many homeowners, the best solution is one of compromise. Consider hiring a contractor to work with you on the initial design and structural evaluation phases of the project and to be in overall control of ordering, scheduling, and inspections. The contractor can also perform the major structural work and any other phases of the construction that you'd rather not tackle. You can then do those portions of the work you're most comfortable with, still save some money in the process, and still have the pride of being involved in the finished product.

A few of the areas where you might wish to get involved that will offer you the greatest potential money savings would be:

- □ Unskilled labor, where the labor rate is high in relation to the material costs. This would include things like demolition work, site cleanup, hauling away debris, and stacking or moving materials.
- □ Other trades where labor is fairly high in relation to materials, such as painting.
- □ Highly skilled trades such as plumbing where the labor rates are the highest.

HIRING A CONTRACTOR

Selecting and hiring a contractor is a process that should be approached with some patience and care. You're looking for someone who's a combination of skilled craftsman and honest businessman, and it needs to be someone you're comfortable working with.

The most obvious place to start is with recommendations from friends. If you know someone who had a contractor work on their house and was satisfied with the work and the price, that might be all you need to know. You might even be comfortable enough that you don't need competitive bids.

Lacking any recommendations, you might wish to contact local lumber or building materials suppliers in your area and ask for recommendations. They know the people who shop in their store, they know how well they pay their bills and how cooperative they are to deal with, and they have something of their own reputation on the line when they make a recommendation. Also, you can contact the local building department for a list of contractors in your area (they'll seldom make recommendations, though), you can check the advertisements in the paper, or you can call the state contractor's board.

Arrange to meet with the contractor at your house. Show him the rooms, discuss your plans and ideas with him, and see what suggestions he might have. If you're dealing with a contractor who was not recommended to you by a friend, ask to see some of his past work. Look at a job or two, talk to the homeowners, and see what kind of feeling you get. You can usually trust your instincts to help guide you to a contractor you can work with.

The Estimate

Give the contractor a set of plans or, if they're not ready yet, at least a detailed description of the work you want to have done. Specify as many details as you can to allow him to work up a price that is accurate. If you are dealing with more than one contractor, give them the same specifications to bid from so that you can easily compare their prices.

When the estimates are ready, read them over carefully. Check to see if all the items you specified are included in the bid. If the contractor has added anything else, which he might have done to give you a more complete bid, ask him to explain those items. Finally, compare the bids against each other to see that both contractors were bidding the same type and quality of material. Don't automatically jump at the lowest bid—it's usually not the bargain you're hoping for.

The Contract

Having selected the contractor and agreed on a price, you will be asked to sign a contract for the work. This is for the protection of both parties involved and is nothing to be afraid of. Read the contract carefully, be certain there are no blank spaces, and check for the following items:

□ The material and labor specifications being contracted for are the same as what was bid. Often, a contractor will simply attach a copy of the original specifications to the contract, making this job easier for you.

□ Be certain the price in the contract is the one you agreed on. Check to see that there is a specific payment schedule that outlines how much each payment will be and tells when it is due.

□ See that estimated start and completion dates have been specified. (A contractor on a job faces a number of potential situations that can play havoc with a schedule—weather delays, illness, material back orders, late subcontractors—so be flexible on the completion date.)

□ See that any items you're going to provide and any labor you're going to perform is also clearly spelled out, along with your time frames for completing these items so that you do not hold up the contractor.

2
Framing the Attic

IF YOUR HOME IS LIKE MOST, THE ATTIC AT THIS POINT IS NOTHING MORE THAN A dusty space enclosed with rough lumber. Seeing a finished room here takes some imagination, and some more planning.

Your first step in getting the attic ready for remodeling is to evaluate the existing structure to determine the attic's size and condition, and to pinpoint any potential problems you might encounter during the project. This will give you a much clearer idea of what you can do with the space and what changes will be necessary along the way.

DEFINING THE COMPONENTS

Take a moment to study the construction of the attic and identify its various structural parts (FIG. 2-1). The following definitions describe the basic components of an attic, not all of which might be present in yours (FIG. 2-2).

Rafter—the angled board that makes up the structure of the roof. The length of the rafter between any supporting boards is known as the rafter's *span*.

Ridge—the main board running the length of the attic at the peak to which the rafters are attached.

Decking (also *sheathing*)—the boards or plywood on top of the rafters to which the roofing shingles are attached.

Ceiling Joists—boards under your feet as you stand in the attic. They form the ceiling structure of the rooms below the attic.

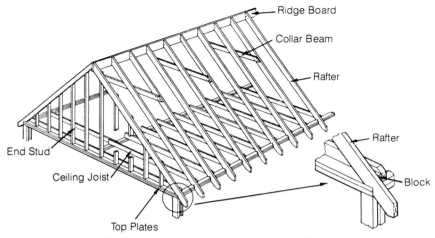

Fig. 2-1. *A typical attic in a home with a gable roof.*

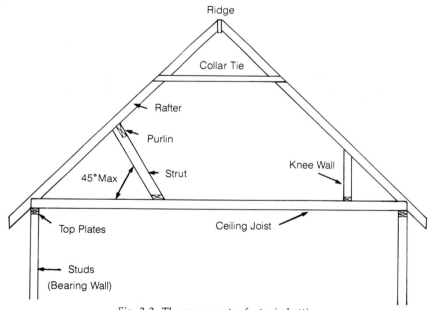

Fig. 2-2. *The components of a typical attic.*

Subfloor—the boards or plywood that cover the tops of the ceiling joists, forming the structural floor of the attic.

Purlin—a horizontal board placed underneath the rafters and at a right angle to them. It is used to shorten the span of the rafter, thereby reducing the size of the lumber that needs to be used for the rafters when the roof is initially framed.

Strut (also *kicker* or *brace*)—board that extends down from the purlin to the attic floor or ceiling joist to support the purlin. Struts must end over a bearing wall and cannot be at an angle of less than 45 degrees off the horizontal.

Collar Tie (also *rafter tie*)—a board installed horizontally between two opposing rafters that prevents the downward load of the roof from spreading the rafters apart. The ends of the rafters must be tied to the ceiling joists, forming a triangle. If the ceiling joists are at right angles to the rafters, however, and this joist/rafter connection cannot be made, collar ties are used. These ties are spaced a minimum of 48 inches on center and are approximately one-third of the way down between the ridge and the attic floor.

Knee Wall—vertical wall that extends from the floor of the attic to the underside of the rafter at some point along the rafter's length. A knee wall is often used when finishing off an attic to define the attic's space and create vertical wall surfaces. It can also be used in place of a purlin to shorten the span of the rafter.

Truss—a manufactured structural component that incorporates the rafters (called *top chords*) and the ceiling joists (called *bottom chords*) into one interconnected unit (FIG. 2-3). Intermediate members, called *webs*, help lock the entire unit together. Under no circumstances can a truss be cut or altered in any way because its strength is derived from the interaction of all its parts.

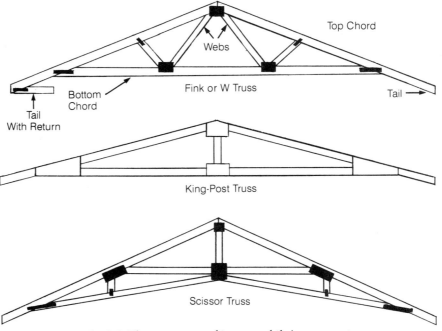

Fig. 2-3. Three common roof trusses and their components.

If your attic was constructed using trusses, it will be impossible to convert it to living space without completely removing the trusses and replacing them with conventional framing.

EVALUATING THE CONDITION OF THE ATTIC

This is a good time to take a close look at the condition of the attic. If there are repairs that need to be made, they can usually be incorporated into the remodeling. Both for scheduling and budgeting purposes, though, you'll want to know about them now.

Look at the condition of the existing rafters. Check their size against the span tables (TABLE 2-1). Are they large enough or can they be supported to shorten their span? Are they structurally sound and free from obvious cracks, warps, or sags? Are they spaced 24 inches or less from center to center, or will additional framing need to be installed to support the drywall?

Examine the ceiling joists and attic floor, if there is one, in the same way. Check the size and span of the joists and the thickness of the material used for the subfloor. Once again, check for obvious structural defects.

Now study the attic with an eye toward obstructions that might affect the new rooms. Will plumbing be in the way, and how and where can it be moved? Are there structural beams or other framing that will need to be moved or incorporated into the new design? Often, a chimney will penetrate the attic space on its way through the roof. Because a chimney is virtually impossible to remove or relocate, can it be made a part of the new room?

Finally, check the condition of the underside of the roof. Is there any daylight showing through from missing shingles or loose flashings? Are there stains or water marks on the rafters or around protruding nail points? Is there any fungus or mold that would indicate moisture problems, either from a leaking roof or from poor ventilation? Any of these might be indicators of problems with the existing roofing, and new shingles might need to be part of your overall remodeling plan.

EVALUATING THE SIZE OF THE ATTIC

It's not always easy at first glance to determine how much room you'll have in the attic when you're finished. The sloping roof has to be taken into consideration, and some of the floor area will not be usable when you're finished remodeling.

Most building codes require you to maintain a minimum finished ceiling height in the attic of $7^1/2$ feet. (Codes in some areas and circumstances allow a finished height as low as 7 feet, so verify this important dimension with your local building department in the early stages of your planning.) The building codes further state that in a room with a sloped ceiling, like an attic, the $7^1/2$-foot minimum height only needs to be maintained over 50 percent of the room's floor area (FIG. 2-4). Only those areas of the room with a finished

Table 2-1. A Standard Span for Rafters.
(Courtesy of Western Wood Products Association)

SPECIES OR GROUP	GRADE*	2 × 6		2 × 8		2 × 10	
		16″ oc	24″ oc	16″ oc	24″ oc	16″ oc	24″ oc
20# Live Load (7 Day), 15# Dead Load							L/240
DOUGLAS	2	13-11	11-5	18-5	15-0	23-6	19-2
FIR-LARCH	3	10-8	8-9	14-1	11-6	17-11	14-8
DOUGLAS	2	12-11	11-0	17-3	14-6	22-8	18-6
FIR SOUTH	3	10-4	8-6	13-8	11-2	17-6	14-3
HEM-FIR	2	12-5	10-2	16-5	13-4	20-11	17-2
	3	9-6	7-9	12-6	10-3	16-0	13-0
WHITE WOODS	2	11-2	9-2	14-9	12-0	18-10	15-4
(Western Woods)	3	8-7	7-0	11-4	9-3	14-6	11-10
30# Live Load (Snow), 15# Dead Load							L/240
DOUGLAS	2	11-10	9-7	15-7	12-9	19-11	16-3
FIR-LARCH	3	9-1	7-4	11-11	9-9	15-3	12-5
DOUGLAS	2	11-4	9-4	15-0	12-3	19-2	15-8
FIR SOUTH	3	8-9	7-2	11-7	9-5	14-9	12-1
HEM-FIR	2	10-6	8-7	13-10	11-4	17-8	14-5
	3	8-1	6-7	10-8	8-8	13-7	11-1
WHITE WOODS	2	9-5	7-8	12-6	10-1	15-10	12-11
(Western Woods)	3	7-3	5-11	9-7	7-10	12-2	10-0
40# Live Load (Snow), 15# Dead Load							L/240
DOUGLAS	2	10-8	8-8	14-1	11-6	18-0	14-8
FIR-LARCH	3	8-2	6-8	10-9	8-10	13-9	11-3
DOUGLAS	2	10-4	8-5	13-7	11-1	17-4	14-2
FIR SOUTH	3	7-11	·6-6	10-5	8-6	13-4	10-11
HEM-FIR	2	9-6	7-9	12-7	10-3	16-0	13-1
	3	7-3	5-11	9-7	7-10	12-3	10-0
WHITE WOODS	2	8-6	6-11	11-3	9-2	14-4	11-8
(Western Woods)	3	6-7	5-4	8-8	7-1	11-1	9-0

*Design Criteria: Spans were computed for commonly marketed grades and species. Spans for other grades and species can be computed utilizing the WWPA Span Computer.
Strength—15 pounds per sq. ft. dead load plus live load indicated in each heading determines required fiber stress.
Deflection—Based on live load only as indicated in each heading and limited to span in inches divided by 240.

Note: The tables are broken into three categories, depending on the estimated load the roof will have to support. *Live load* is the weight of snow, ice, or other changeable factors. *Dead load* is the weight of the framing itself.

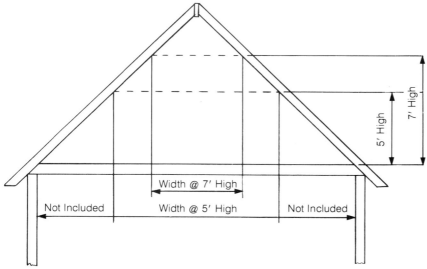

Fig. 2-4. Calculating head room in an attic. The square footage of the 7-foot high section must be at least 50 percent of the square footage of the 5-foot high section.

wall height of 5 feet or more count toward the measurement of the room's square footage—the remaining area is ignored for this calculation.

To make these calculations, first measure from the floor of the attic to the underside of the rafters to determine the point where you have $7\frac{1}{2}$ feet of head room. Remember that this is *finished* head room, so be sure and allow for the thickness of the subfloor, underlayment, and finished flooring you'll be installing, plus the thickness of the drywall on the ceiling. Also, if you'll be installing larger floor joists (see "Floor Joists" later in this chapter), you'll need to allow for their height also.

After you've marked the rafters at $7\frac{1}{2}$ feet, use a plumb bob or a long level and mark the point on the floor directly below the rafter marks. Measure between these points and make a note of that dimension. Now repeat the procedure at the 5-foot height, making a note of this measurement also. Finally, measure the length of the attic.

Now some simple multiplication is all that's needed. For example, suppose your attic is a total of 30 feet long and, at the point where the walls are 5 feet high, it is 26 feet wide. Multiply 26 by 30, and you'll see that you have a total of 780 square feet of floor area with a minimum finished ceiling height of 5 feet. Now, if the attic is 20 feet wide at the point where the walls are $7\frac{1}{2}$ feet high, you'll have 600 square feet of floor area with a minimum finished ceiling height of $7\frac{1}{2}$ feet. Because 600 square feet is more than 50 percent of 780 square feet, this attic would meet the building code requirements.

INCREASING THE HEAD ROOM

If your calculations have determined that the attic does not have sufficient head room, there are a variety of ways to correct this. In many cases, the collar ties present the only problem because they are usually installed below where you want the ceiling. The obvious temptation is to simply remove them, but they do form an important part of the roof's structural integrity.

If you are only lacking 4 or 5 inches of ceiling height, the building inspectors will often let you move the collar ties up a little higher on the rafters. This still offers you the structural support you need, while forming a horizontal surface between the rafters to attach the finished ceiling to.

Another solution is to replace the collar ties with some other form of structural support for the rafters. Remember that the collar ties are needed only when the lower ends of the rafters are not tied to the ceiling joists. If the rafters can be tied to something else, then the collar ties can be taken out. This is usually done by installing new attic floor joists that run parallel to the rafters on the same spacing, then simply attaching the ends of the rafters to the ends of the new joists.

One of the most popular ways of gaining needed head room is by installing dormers (FIG. 2-5), which also give you the opportunity to add windows for light and ventilation. For more information on dormers and their construction, see chapter 3.

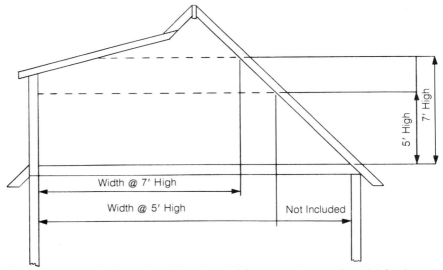

Fig. 2-5. *An example of how the addition of a shed dormer can increase the attic's head room.* (COURTESY OF WESTERN WOOD PRODUCTS ASSOCIATION)

Another possibility, although it's one to be considered only as a last resort, is to lower the ceiling of the rooms below the attic. This solution requires a considerable amount of additional framing to reconstruct the structural triangle formed by the rafters and the ceiling joists. It is obviously practical only when the ceiling heights of the downstairs rooms are tall enough to accommodate lowering.

FLOOR JOISTS

All too often, the original ceiling joists that were installed to support the ceiling material of the rooms below are inadequate to act as floor joists for the new attic rooms. Floor joists must support a considerably greater amount of weight than the ceiling joists do, and so must be sized accordingly.

Referring to the span table in TABLE 2-2, determine the size of the floor joists that will be necessary to span the width of your attic. For example, if your attic is 20 feet wide, you would need to have 2-×-12 joists on 16-inch centers to span that distance. On the other hand, that same attic only requires 2 × 8s on 24-inch centers to act as ceiling joists.

If the existing ceiling joists (TABLE 2-3) are not large enough to act as floor joists, you have three options open to you to correct the situation: reduce the span of the joists, decrease the spacing between the joists, or install new joists.

Reducing the Span. Even if the attic is 20 feet wide, there is probably a bearing wall somewhere below the attic over which the ceiling joists are split or supported. If, for example, the wall is centered below the attic (FIG. 2-6), the span for the floor joists is now reduced to 10 feet, and the joist size can be reduced to 2 × 8s on 24-inch centers.

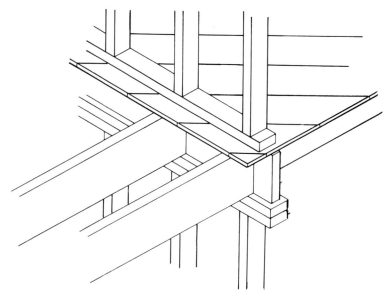

Fig. 2-6. Floor joists are split over a bearing wall to reduce their span.

Table 2-2. Standard Floor Joist Span Table.
(Courtesy of Western Wood Products Association)

SPAN FEET-INCHES

40# Live Load, 10# Dead Load — L/360

SPECIES OR GROUP	GRADE*	2×6 12" oc	2×6 16" oc	2×6 24" oc	2×8 12" oc	2×8 16" oc	2×8 24" oc	2×10 12" oc	2×10 16" oc	2×10 24" oc	2×12 12" oc	2×12 16" oc	2×12 24" oc
DOUGLAS FIR-LARCH	2	10-11	9-11	8-6	14-4	13-1	11-3	18-4	16-9	14-5	22-4	20-4	17-6
	3	9-3	8-0	6-6	12-2	10-7	8-8	15-7	13-6	11-0	18-11	15-5	13-5
DOUGLAS FIR SOUTH	2	10-0	9-1	7-11	13-2	12-0	10-6	16-9	15-3	13-4	20-5	18-7	16-3
	3	9-0	7-9	6-4	11-9	10-3	8-4	15-1	13-1	10-8	18-4	15-11	13-0
HEM-FIR	2	10-3	9-4	7-7	13-6	12-3	10-0	17-3	15-8	12-10	20-11	19-1	15-7
	3	8-3	7-2	5-10	10-10	9-5	7-8	13-10	12-0	9-10	16-10	14-7	11-11
MOUNTAIN HEMLOCK-HEM-FIR	2	9-5	8-7	7-6	12-5	11-4	9-11	15-11	14-6	12-8	19-4	17-7	15-4
	3	8-3	7-2	5-10	10-10	9-5	7-8	13-10	12-0	9-10	16-10	14-7	11-11
WESTERN HEMLOCK	2	10-3	9-4	7-11	13-6	12-3	10-6	17-3	15-8	13-4	20-11	19-1	16-3
	3	8-8	7-6	6-1	11-5	9-11	8-1	14-7	12-8	10-4	17-9	15-5	12-7
ENGELMANN SPRUCE LODGEPOLE PINE (Englemann Spruce-Alpine Fir)	2	9-5	8-7	6-11	12-5	11-2	9-1	15-11	14-3	11-7	19-4	17-3	14-2
	3	7-5	6-5	5-3	9-9	8-6	6-11	12-6	10-10	8-10	15-3	13-2	10-9
LODGEPOLE PINE	2	9-8	8-10	7-3	12-10	11-8	9-7	16-4	14-11	12-3	19-10	18-1	14-11
	3	7-10	6-10	5-7	10-5	9-1	7-5	13-4	11-7	9-5	16-3	14-1	11-6
PONDEROSA PINE-LODGEPOLE PINE	2	9-5	8-7	7-0	12-5	11-4	9-3	15-11	14-5	11-9	19-4	17-7	14-4
	3	7-7	6-6	5-4	10-0	8-8	7-1	12-9	11-1	9-1	15-7	13-6	11-0
WESTERN CEDARS	2	9-2	8-4	7-3	12-0	11-0	9-7	15-4	14-0	12-3	18-9	17-0	14-11
	3	7-10	6-10	5-6	10-5	9-1	7-5	13-4	11-6	9-5	16-3	14-0	11-6
WHITE WOODS (Western Woods)	2	9-2	8-4	6-10	12-0	11-0	9-0	15-5	14-0	11-6	18-9	17-0	14-0
	3	7-5	6-5	5-3	9-9	8-6	6-11	12-6	10-10	8-10	15-3	13-2	10-9

*Design Criteria: Spans were computed for commonly marketed grades. Spans for other grades can be computed utilizing the WWPA Span Computer.
Strength—10 lbs. per sq. ft. dead load plus 40 lbs. per sq. ft. live load.
Deflection—Limited to span in inches divided by 360 for live load only.

Table 2-3. Standard Ceiling Joist Span Table.
(Courtesy of Western Wood Products Association)

		2 × 4			2 × 6		2 × 8	
SPECIES OR GROUP	GRADE*	16" oc	24" oc	GRADE*	16" oc	24" oc	16" oc	24" oc
								L/240
		10# Live Load (No Storage), 5# Dead Load						
DOUGLAS FIR-LARCH	STD	8-3	6-9	2	18-1	15-7	23-10	20-7
				3	14-8	11-11	19-4	15-9
DOUGLAS FIR SOUTH	STD	8-1	6-8	2	16-6	14-5	21-9	19-0
				3	14-2	11-7	18-9	15-3
HEM-FIR	STD	7-6	6-1	2	16-11	13-11	22-4	18-4
				3	13-1	10-8	17-2	14-0
MOUNTAIN HEMLOCK-HEM-FIR	STD	7-8	6-2	2	15-7	13-8	20-7	18-0
				3	13-1	10-8	17-2	14-0
WESTERN HEMLOCK	STD	7-10	6-4	2	16-11	14-6	22-4	19-1
				3	13-9	11-3	18-1	14-10
ENGELMANN SPRUCE-LODGEPOLE PINE (Englemann Spruce Alpine Fir)	STD	6-9	5-6	2	15-6	12-8	20-7	16-8
				3	11-9	9-7	15-6	12-8
LODGEPOLE PINE	STD	7-1	5-10	2	16-1	13-3	21-2	17-6
				3	12-7	10-3	16-7	13-6
PONDEROSA PINE-LODGEPOLE PINE	STD	6-9	5-6	2	15-7	12-10	20-7	16-10
				3	12-0	9-10	15-10	12-11
WESTERN CEDARS	STD	7-1	5-10	2	15-1	13-2	20-0	17-6
				3	12-7	10-3	16-7	13-7
WHITE WOODS (Western Woods)	STD	6-7	5-4	2	15-1	12-6	20-2	16-5
				3	11-9	9-8	15-6	12-8

SPAN FEET-INCHES

*Design Criteria: Spans were computed for commonly marketed grades. Spans for other grades can be computed utilizing the WWPA Span Computer.
Strength—5 lbs. per sq. ft. dead load plus 10 lbs. per sq. ft. live load. No storage above.
Deflection—Limited to span in inches divided by 240 for live load only.

Study the layout of your house carefully. Determine what bearing walls might exist that could help you reduce the span of the floor joists. You will need to check under the house to see how the foundation and piers were laid out to be certain which walls are load-bearing.

If you encounter an interior wall that is in a good location to support the joists but is not currently a load-bearing wall, you might be able to place new piers under it to make it fully load-bearing. Check with your building department for the specific pier requirements.

Decreasing the Spacing. Another alternative is to decrease the spacing between the existing ceiling joists. For example, if the existing ceiling joists are 2 × 8s on 24-inch centers, they would only span $11^{1/4}$ feet when used as floor joists. Adding another 2 × 8 between the existing ones would reduce the spacing to 12 inches on center and would now allow them to span $14^{1/3}$ feet.

Installing New Floor Joists. In many cases, the only alternative is to install new lumber that is the correct size to act as floor joists for a given span. Once again, refer to the span table to determine the proper size lumber you'll need. Remember that if you can support the joists at an intermediate point and reduce the overall span, you can also reduce the size of the lumber you'll need to use.

STRENGTHENING THE FOUNDATION

Your home's foundation consists of two elements: the footing and the stem wall. The *footing* is designed to spread the weight of the house out over a wide area of ground. The *stem wall* raises the house above the ground and creates the open area, called a *crawl space*, beneath the first floor. In a house with a basement, the stem walls are made taller and become the walls of the basement.

Footings and stem walls are designed to support a certain load and are sized according to how many stories the home has. Converting your attic into living space is essentially the same as adding another story to the house, and the foundation will need to be adequately sized to support the additional load.

Refer to TABLE 2-4 for common footing and stem-wall sizes, then check the size of the foundation that currently exists for your home. If the foundation was oversized when it was originally poured and is large enough to support the new room (for example, you have a one-story house but the footings were sized for two stories), then no additional strengthening is necessary. If, however, the foundation is not currently large enough for the additional living space in the attic, the building department might require that you strengthen it in some manner.

There are several ways of strengthening the foundation, depending on the situation. Perhaps the easiest is to excavate a trench around the house

Table 2-4. Comparison of the Footing and Stem-Wall Sizes Required For One-, Two-, or Three-Story Houses.

Number of Stories	Footing Width	Depth	Stemwall Width
1	12	6	6
2	15	7	8
3	18	8	10

alongside the existing footings. Drill holes in the old footings and insert steel reinforcing bars, called *rebar*, into the holes. Place additional rebar in the trench and tie them to the rebar in the footings, then fill the trench with concrete to widen and strengthen the old footing.

It might also be possible to pour new piers under the house. Pour concrete columns, called *buttresses*, at intermediate points along the outside of the old foundation to provide additional lateral support.

All of these techniques require the prior approval of the building department. The work should be designed and sized by a competent engineer or building contractor prior to construction.

FRAMING THE ATTIC

With the preliminary evaluations and measurements completed, revise your design as necessary to accommodate the actual conditions found in the attic. It's now time to begin the construction of the new rooms.

Floor Joists

If your evaluations determined that new floor joists are necessary, their installation will be your first step (FIG. 2-7). As you will soon learn, one of the biggest problems with the new joists is simply getting them into the attic! You might want to open up a strip of roofing and roof sheathing at the attic floor level, and slide the new joists in from outside. This method also facilitates nailing the new joists to the plates. Another method is to open up the roof where you'll be installing a dormer or skylight, and bring the joists in through there. In either case, precut the joists to length and angle the ends as necessary to match the rafters before you bring the joists into the attic.

In most cases, you will find it easiest to simply place the new floor joists in between the existing ceiling joists. Remember, though, that if you are removing existing collar ties and intend to replace them in the roof's structural triangle by attaching the new floor joists to the rafters, then you will have to position the joists next to the rafters and nail them together.

Place 2-×-4 blocking flat on top of the exterior wall plates first, between the ceiling joists. Also, place similar blocking on top of any intermediate bearing walls that will be supporting any of the new floor joist load.

Fig. 2-7. *Two examples of how new floor joists are installed over the existing, undersized ceiling joists. Note the metal safety plates used over the holes where the pipes are to prevent damage when the subfloor is nailed down.*

Place the new floor joists on the blocking and toenail them in place. This raises the joists 1½ inches above the old ceiling, enabling them to clear much of the existing electrical wiring, plumbing, and other obstructions. Also, this isolates the joists from the old ceiling to reduce noise transmission, and lessens the chance that nailing the joists into place will crack the existing ceiling material, an especially important consideration if the old ceiling is made of plaster.

Wiring, Plumbing, and Insulation

After the joists have been installed, complete any electrical wiring, plumbing (FIGS. 2-8 through 2-10), or heating duct work that needs to be concealed in the floor. Also, it is strongly recommended that you place insulation between the floor joists prior to installing the subfloor. The insulation will deaden the sound transmitted between the stories.

Fig. 2-8. *The new, deeper floor joists will accommodate the under-floor plumbing in this attic bathroom more readily than the shallower ceiling joists.*

Subflooring

The next step is to cover the new floor joists (or the old ceiling joists if they're strong enough to be acting as floor joists) with subflooring. This will create the floor for the new rooms and give you a base for subsequent framing.

Fig. 2-9. An example of how the new ABS plastic plumbing pipes are connected to the old cast iron, using the rubber sleeve and clamps at the transition point (lower center). This is known as a band clamp or no-hub fitting.

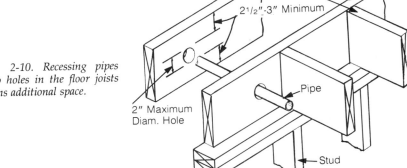

Fig. 2-10. Recessing pipes into holes in the floor joists gains additional space.

If the access is adequate to get them into the attic, the easiest subflooring material to work with is 4- × -8-foot plywood sheets. These should be a minimum of ⁵/₈ inch thick (³/₄ inch preferred) and have tongue-and-groove edges for strength. There are also a number of good waferboard and oriented strand board products on the market, also in 4- × -8-foot tongue-and-groove sheets, that are a little less expensive.

Lay the long dimension of the sheets perpendicular to the joists, making certain that each sheet begins and ends over the center of a joist. Stagger the seams for greatest strength, which is easily accomplished by beginning the first row with a full sheet, then the second row with a half sheet, then back to a full sheet, etc. Nail the sheets to the floor joists with 6d or 8d ring shank nails on 8-inch centers. Also, applying a bead of construction adhesive to the tops of the joists before installing the subfloor will increase its strength and eliminate squeaks in the floor.

The subfloor only needs to extend past the line where the knee walls will be, if desired. If you plan to use the area behind the knee walls for storage, then install the subfloor all the way out to the exterior wall plates.

Knee Walls

Knee walls, while not always necessary from a structural standpoint, are a part of almost every attic conversion. Knee walls create a vertical boundary around the room that provides a place to install electrical outlets and plumbing, and a surface to place furniture against. They also simplify adding insulation and lessen the amount of room space that needs to be heated. Finally, knee walls create a small, wedge-shaped space behind them that is ideal for enclosed storage.

As discussed previously, knee walls are usually placed at the point where the rafters are 5 feet above the attic floor. This 5-foot height, in addition to being one of the guidelines for measuring the attic as established by the building code, is also a good height for most furniture and keeps the room feeling open and uncramped. You can place the knee walls at other heights, but it is suggested that they not be less than 4 feet in height.

Begin the wall layout at one end of the attic. Using a plumb bob or a board and a level, establish a vertical line at the correct wall height and mark both the rafter and the subfloor. Repeat this procedure at the other end of the attic, again marking both the rafter and the subfloor. Snap a chalk line through both sets of points.

Using the chalk line as a guide, nail a 2-×-4 sole plate to the subfloor. Make certain the line is against the front of the 2 × 4, then use 16d nails through the plate into the floor joists.

The studs can be installed in one of three ways (FIG. 2-11):

1. You can rip a 2 × 6 on an angle to act as a top plate, attach it to the underside of the rafters along the chalk line, then attach the studs to it.
2. You can run the studs alongside each rafter and face-nail them in place, then block between them.
3. You can cut the studs on an angle, toenail them to the rafters, then block between them.

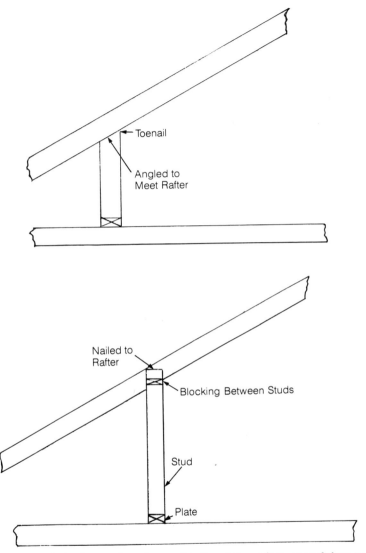

Fig. 2-11. Two methods of connecting a knee wall to the existing rafters: an angled cut toenailed to the rafters (top); and studs nailed to the sides of the rafters (bottom).

Openings in the knee walls are constructed like any other wall openings, using king studs and trimmers to support a doubled 2-×-4 or 2-×-6 header that spans the opening. The tops of the header boards must be cut on an angle to match the slope of the roof.

Ceiling Joists

If you want the ceiling of the new room to follow the underside of the rafters all the way to the ridge, then installing ceiling joists is not necessary. In many cases, however, the use of ceiling joists to create a more conventional flat ceiling has several advantages: a painted, flat ceiling is brighter and eliminates shadows at the peak; light fixtures are easier to install; and, if the attic is particularly tall, the amount of area to heat is less.

Installing the ceiling joists is quite simple. First, select the ceiling height, bearing in mind the minimum ceiling heights discussed earlier. Use a level to mark across each pair of opposing rafters at the correct height, then cut 2-×-4 or 2-×-6 lumber (depending on the span) to the correct length and angle. Use 16d nails to face-nail the joists to the sides of the rafters.

Partition Walls

To further divide the interior space you've created with the knee walls and ceiling joists, you can install partition walls (FIG. 2-12). These walls are not load-bearing, and can be placed anywhere in the room.

Fig. 2-12. *Partition wall framing (left) in a new shed dormer. Note storage area created behind dormer side wall framing (center).*

Mark out the floor where you wish the walls to go and snap chalk lines to guide the placement of the sole plates. Cut the plates to length and nail them to the subfloor along the lines. Use a plumb bob to establish vertical lines between the sole plate and the underside of the ceiling joists, then mark chalk lines across these points. If the wall is perpendicular to the ceiling joists, the top plate can simply be nailed to the joists. If the wall and the joists are parallel (FIGS. 2-13 and 2-14) and the wall falls in between two joists, block between the joists and secure the top plate to the blocking. Finally, install the studs by toenailing them to the top and bottom plates, checking each one for plumb as you install them.

Fig. 2-13. Securing a partition wall that runs parallel to the ceiling joists, using cross blocking between the joists.

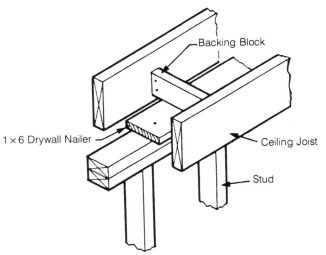

Fig. 2-14. A similar method of attaching partition walls, with the addition of a 1-×-6 nailer to attach the drywall sheets to.

GABLE ENDS

Another important attic area not to be overlooked is the gable end wall. This triangular-shaped area is often quite large and is an ideal place for windows. Large windows in this area can be quite striking, and the high vantage point often offers a beautiful view.

Many gable ends already have a small window in them, but the size can easily be increased for maximum light, ventilation, and appearance. Triangular windows, used alone or paired with standard square or rectangular windows, offer some great possibilities (FIG. 2-15). Match the angle of the window to the angle of the rafter for best appearance. Below those you can install additional rectangular windows of the same width. These lower windows should be operable to take advantage of the natural convective air flow.

Fig. 2-15. *A nice gable window arrangement for light and ventilation. The triangular windows are matched to the slope of the rafters.*

3
Constructing Dormers

ONE OF THE MOST COMMON AND EFFECTIVE WAYS OF GAINING HEAD ROOM IN AN attic, as well as additional light (FIG. 3-1), ventilation, and floor space, is through the addition of a dormer. A *dormer* is simply a projection that is cut and framed into the existing roof and houses one or more windows in its end wall. For even more light, triangular windows can be installed in the dormer's side walls.

Because it is framed perpendicular to the old roof, the dormer increases the head room of the attic in that area and provides more usable floor space. Also, those portions of the dormer that have walls higher than 5 feet can be used in the total floor space calculations described in chapter 2, which might make the difference between an attic that meets the building codes for ceiling height and one that doesn't (see FIGS. 2-4 and 2-5 in chapter 2).

DORMER CONFIGURATIONS

Dormers can be constructed in a variety of configurations (FIG. 3-2). They might be only a few feet wide, or they might take up the entire length of the house. Some types require some tricky framing, but most are within the skill range of the experienced do-it-yourselfer.

Dormers are named for the type of roof configuration they have. The two most common types are the gable dormer and the shed dormer.

(COURTESY OF VELUX-AMERICA INC.)

Fig. 3-1. Operable skylights in the open-beam roof of a new shed dormer.

Gable Dormers

Gable dormers are relatively small and have a double-sloping roof that intersects the existing roof at a right angle. It is this intersection that gives the gable dormer its charm and architectural appeal, but it is also the limiting factor in its size. As the dormer gets wider, the ridge has to get higher, until you finally reach a point where the ridge of the dormer's roof is taller than the ridge of the home's main roof. To compensate for its comparatively narrow width, several gable dormers might be placed in a row along the same side of the building.

Gable dormers get their name from having a gable end, which is fairly easy to match to the existing house. There are some offshoots of the gable configuration. Most notable is the *hip dormer*, which has the same type of framing and size limitations but is topped with a hip roof. Other types include the *curved roof*, which has a gable end wall but a curved roof; the *eyebrow*, a feature on some older styles of homes which consists of little more than a window sticking up above the roofline with a slightly curved roof; and the *light scoop*, which is similar to the eyebrow but has a flat roof.

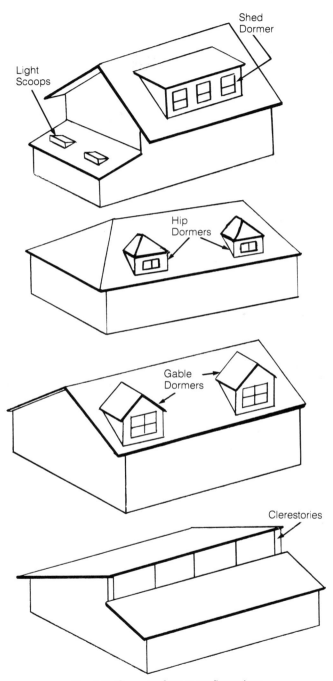

Fig. 3-2. Common dormer configurations.

Shed Dormers

Easier to construct and offering greater interior space, the shed dormer is often the choice for attic remodelers. Unlike the gable dormer, the shed roof has only a single slope with no ridge. Its roof begins near the ridge of the existing roof, and slants downward at a relatively shallow slope, usually no greater than 4 in 12.

As a result of this roof configuration, the shed dormer can be as wide as you would like it—in fact, narrower ones tend to look a little awkward. Most cover at least one-third to one-half of the home's length, and many extend the entire length of the roof.

PREPARING THE ATTIC FOR THE DORMER

No matter what type of dormer you intend to construct, they all have one basic thing in common—they require a hole in the home's existing roof. After the hole is laid out and cut, the existing roof framing is reinforced, then the dormer is actually constructed on and around the framing that surrounds the opening.

Laying Out the Dormer

The first step in the dormer's construction is to determine and lay out the size you want. There are several determining factors: how much floor space you'd like to gain; how much head room you need; where the dormer will fall in the interior layout of each attic room; how the dormer will lay out relative to the outside appearance of the house, and whether or not it will need to be centered to a particular area; the configuration of the existing framing; and any chimneys or other obstacles you might need to avoid.

The type of dormer you wish to construct will also affect its positioning in the attic. When framing a gable dormer, all three of the walls are bearing part of the roof load. The small size and comparatively light loads, however, will generally permit you to frame the dormer directly on top of doubled roof rafters, with no additional reinforcing.

With the shed dormer, the bulk of the load is placed on the front wall, which has all of the rafters resting on it. As such, you'll need to place the shed dormer's front wall directly over one of the home's existing bearing walls, usually the exterior wall (FIG. 3-3), or else reinforce the attic floor underneath this front wall. It's best to discuss your plans with the building department to get their recommendations before proceeding with the framing.

Begin the layout by marking the dimensions of the dormer on the attic floor. If possible, try to have the edges of the layout coincide with existing rafters to simplify the framing. Next, use a plumb bob (FIG. 3-4) to transfer those layout marks to the rafters and the underside of the roof. At each corner of the layout, drive a 16d nail up through the roof sheathing so that it is visible from on top of the roof.

Fig. 3-3. A large shed dormer under construction. The front wall of the dormer is directly over the load-bearing exterior wall of the house, transferring the dormer's weight down to the foundation.

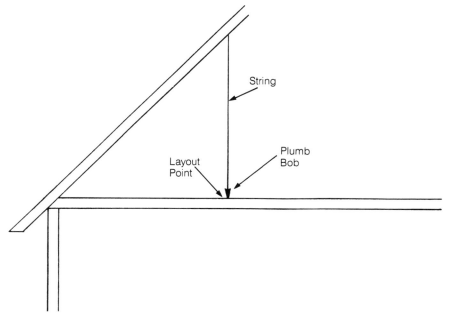

Fig. 3-4. Use a plumb bob and line to transfer marks between the ceiling and the floor.

Doubling the Side Rafters

You will now need to double up the rafters at each side of the opening, which is done to provide the necessary structural strength to bear the additional loads. In the case of some larger types of shed dormers, the building inspectors might even require that the rafters be tripled.

Select straight, solid lumber that is the same dimension as the existing rafters. Check each board carefully for *crown* (a curve along the length of the board). If one is present, lay out the rafter so that the crown will be up. In this way, the weight of the roof will press down against the crown and straighten it out, rather than causing it to sag further.

Place the body of an adjustable bevel gauge against the underside of one of the existing rafters, then align the tongue with the side of the ridge board. This will give you the angle for the plumb cut on the end of the new rafter. Measure the overall length of the rafter, mark the bevel on the other end so that it matches the plate or ceiling joist (depending on where the new rafter will sit), and cut the new rafter accordingly.

Set the bottom end of the rafter in place, then swing the rafter up to the ridge and against the side of the existing rafter. Use 16d nails to secure the two rafters together.

Stripping the Roofing

Before beginning the demolition process of the old roofing, you must provide temporary bracing under the rafters. The bracing is designed to carry the weight of the roof during construction so that nothing sags as the existing structural members are cut and removed.

Mark the rafters about 12 inches up from where the opening will be, then measure down to the floor of the attic. This will determine the height of the temporary wall you'll need to construct. Cut two 2-×-4 plates long enough to extend past the opening on each side, then cut enough 2 × 4s to make studs 24 inches on center. Working flat on the attic floor, construct the wall, then tilt it up into position. Nail the plates to both the rafters and the attic floor to ensure that the temporary wall doesn't move. Repeat this procedure for the short wall at the bottom side of the opening.

Next, you'll need to go up on the roof and strip off the existing shingles. If the roof is steeper than 8 in 12, or steeper than you're comfortable working on without support, take the time to rig safety ropes or a temporary working platform. Most rental yards stock steel roof brackets, which are nailed temporarily to the rafters and hold a 2 × 6 to act as a platform for you and your tools.

Using the nails you installed earlier as a guide to the location of the dormer, begin stripping off the roofing. Remove enough shingles to expose an area about 12 to 16 inches wider than the opening on all sides.

Using a chalk line, snap a line between the nails to mark the cutout in the sheathing. Cut along these lines, using an electric circular saw with the blade set to the thickness of the sheathing. Remove and discard the sheathing.

FRAMING THE ROOF OPENING

You will now need to cut and remove the rafters from inside the opening (FIG. 3-5). Remember that those portions of the rafter from the ridge down to the opening and from the plate up to the opening will remain in place and become part of the new structure, so make your cuts cleanly and carefully. A reciprocating saw, which can be rented if you don't own one, will work best in this situation, or you can use a handsaw.

How the rafters are cut, as well as some of the subsequent framing procedures, depends on what type of dormer you are framing. You will find that the shed dormer is considerably easier to construct because of the lack of intersecting angles.

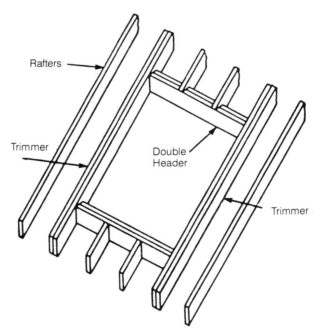

Fig. 3-5. *Typical roof framing configuration for a dormer opening. Note the doubled trimmers at the sides of the opening and the doubled headers at the top and bottom, which bear the weight of the cut rafters.*

Framing a Shed Dormer Opening

You will need to mark and cut the rafters at the top of the opening so that they are square to the ends of the dormer's rafters (FIG. 3-6). The easiest way

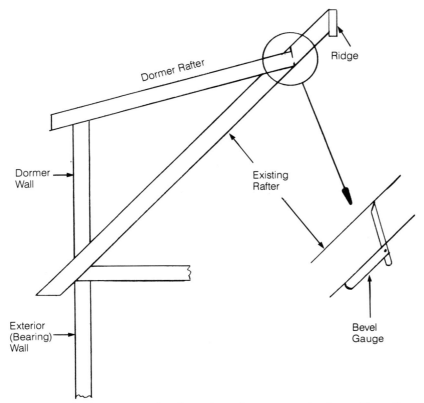

Fig. 3-6. Use a bevel gauge to mark and transfer angle measurements when cutting rafters.

to do this is to take a long piece of straight lumber and place it in the opening, against the joists. Position it as if it were one of the new rafters so that it is located at the correct height and is sitting at the proper angle for the roof pitch you have selected, then temporarily secure it to the old rafters with C-clamps. Carefully double-check and adjust the positioning, then mark the angle of the board against the side of the rafter. This will give you a line to set your bevel gauge against. Mark and cut each of the old rafters at the top.

The bottoms of the rafters receive a *plumb cut,* meaning that the cut is vertical. You can mark these cuts using the bevel guage or with a level. Have a helper hold each rafter in turn as you make the second cut so that the cut section does not bind or fall and damage the ceiling below. Remove and discard each section.

Use 2× lumber to frame a double header across the top and bottom of the opening. First, cut four pieces to span the distance between the doubled rafters on each side of the opening. Place the first one across the cut ends of the rafters at the top of the opening, then nail the header board to each of the rafters. Install the second header board against the first, nailing the two together with 16d nails.

Using prefabricated steel joist hangers, secure the ends of the header to the doubled side joists. You can use 3-inch wide hangers, although these are sometimes difficult to find and might have to be ordered. An alternative is to use standard 3¹/2-inch hangers, which are made to accommodate 4× lumber. Simply add a small section of ¹/4-inch plywood on each side to fill out the hanger.

Repeat the double header and joist hanger installation on the bottom of the opening. Once both headers are complete and secure, you can remove the temporary walls you constructed earlier.

Framing a Gable Dormer Opening

The procedure for marking and sawing the bottom cut on the old rafters is the same for a gable dormer as it was for a shed dormer. Simply mark each one for a plumb cut (vertical line), then make the cut with a handsaw or reciprocating saw.

For the top of the opening, two different methods can be used. If the dormer is fairly small, you can temporarily tack pieces of lumber vertically to the rafters in line with where the end wall will be. From there, you can use a level to project back up the roof and mark exactly where the plates of the side walls will meet the doubled side rafters. Next, establish the ridge height at the temporary end wall, then project back to mark where the ridge will intersect the existing roof.

Measure back 1¹/2 inches from the ridge point and mark the rafter at that point for a plumb cut. Cut and remove that one rafter section, then frame a single header between the adjacent rafters on each side. Nail the header off to the side rafters and to the end of the cut rafter.

Next, snap a chalk line between your mark on the side wall plate and the point of the ridge. These lines will indicate where each subsequent rafter needs to be cut off to receive the new valley rafter. These cuts will be on a *compound angle*, meaning that the cut is angled both top to bottom and across the face of the board. You will find this easiest to do with an electric circular saw. Set the blade on an angle that corresponds to the mark you made across the top of the rafter (you can measure this with your bevel gauge), then cut down the rafter on a plumb-cut angle.

Remove and discard each cut section of rafter. Measure and cut the valley rafter on each side, which will again require a compound angle cut at each end. Install the valley rafters by nailing them to the top header, to the cut ends of each rafter, and to the doubled side rafter. Install a doubled header at the bottom of the opening as described in the shed dormer section, or if you will be framing the end wall directly on top of the bottom header, use a piece of 4× lumber instead of the doubled 2×s to simplify your framing alignment. Fiinally, remove the temporary walls.

If the gable dormer you are building is relatively large and extends up the roof fairly close to the ridge, the alternative framing method is to first cut each rafter at the bottom of the opening, then remove the cut sections all the way up to the ridge. Framing in the top header and valley rafters proceeds as described, but this frmaing method allows you to cut and install the jack rafters out of new lumber instead of trying to accurately cut off the old ones in place.

FRAMING THE DORMER

Once the roofing and sheathing have been removed, and the opening is complete, the rest of the dormer's framing can be done from the floor of the attic. You can bring your lumber and other materials in through the opening and stack them in the attic for future use. You might even want to use this opportunity to bring in bulky fixtures, such as one-piece shower stalls, or perhaps even large furniture pieces.

Shed Roof Dormer

As discussed earlier, the front wall of a shed dormer is longer and carries more of the roof's load than the front wall of a gable dormer. It must be constructed, therefore, over a bearing wall, usually one of the home's existing exterior walls. This actually simplifies the framing because the walls are built flat on the attic floor and then tilted up into position, as is done with regular wall framing (FIG. 3-7).

Fig. 3-7. Wall and rafter framing details for a shed dormer.

Begin by cutting two 2-×-4 plates to the proper length—one to the actual length of the opening and one that is 7 inches longer. Using conventional framing methods, construct the wall so that the top plate overhangs the end studs by 3¹/2 inches at each end. Frame for the window openings using a conventional king stud/trimmer/header arrangement. Long walls might need to be framed in two or more sections for ease of handling.

With a helper, tilt the wall up and move it into the opening. (You might have to move it at a slight angle to swing the overhanging top plate into place.) Push the wall against the opening's bottom header, plumb the wall, then nail it in place through the bottom plate into the attic floor and by toe-nailing the studs to the opening header. Long or tall walls might need some temporary bracing until the rafters are installed.

Install the bottom plates for the two side walls by nailing them directly to the doubled rafters at each side of the opening. Cut and install the outside corners next, using either doubled 2 × 4s with a spacer in between to make the corner 3¹/2 inches wide or simply a 4-×-4 post. Finally, install the second top plate.

The next step is to install the rafters. Cut each rafter to length. Use a square cut at the end that will butt against the opening's top header. Use a plumb, square, or decorative cut at the other end, depending on the look you desire for the finished overhang. Set one rafter in place at the side of the dormer, mark and cut the bird's-mouth, then check the rafter for proper fit. Using this one as a pattern, cut and install all the rafters.

Finish the framing by cutting and installing the side wall studs (FIGS. 3-8 and 3-9). Each stud will be a different length as you work your way up the slope of the roof and will require a beveled cut at the bottom and a 1¹/2-inch-deep notch at the top fit around the rafter. Toenail the stud to the plate at the bottom and directly to the rafter at the top. Install an outside rafter at the top of each side wall to create a small overhang over the walls, or use lookouts, brackets, or other standard framing techniques to create a wider side overhang.

Gable or Hip Roof Dormer

The gable dormer's end wall can be constructed in the same manner as the one for the shed dormer. Because of their relatively small size, however, they are usually just framed directly on top of the opening (FIG. 3-10).

Because the bottom header of the opening was installed against the plumb cuts of the rafters, the top of the header is now horizontal, so the end wall studs can be cut off square. Simply cut the studs to length, toenail them onto the header, and then install a top plate. Use conventional framing to construct the window openings.

Construct the side walls next, either by installing a bottom plate on top of the doubled side rafters or by framing directly on top of the rafters. Bevel cut

Fig. 3-8. *Shed dormer side wall framing with window opening. Partition walls will enclose a new bathroom.*

Fig. 3-9. *Framing a new attic window into an existing wall, above the roof of the story below.*

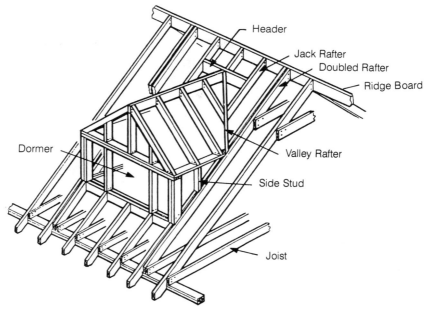

Fig. 3-10. Typical gable dormer framing details.

the bottom of each stud, toenail it in place, then install the top plate. Complete the wall framing by doubling the top plate on all three walls, overlapping the corners.

The roof is now constructed using conventional framing methods. Install the ridge at the proper height, cut and bird's-mouth the rafters, then frame the gable end wall between the top plate and the rafters. Frame and install any overhangs as desired.

THE FINISHING TOUCHES

The construction of the dormer is finished off to match the existing architectural style of the house as closely as possible to avoid a "tacked on" look. Sheath the walls and roof with plywood, then install the new windows. Install siding last, after the roofing has been completed, so that the new siding overlaps the flashings used when patching in the shingles.

Care must be taken when roofing the dormer and patching in the shingles on the old roof (FIG. 3-11). Use the proper type of valley flashing (FIG. 3-12) or shingle weaving in the valleys, and step flashing where the shingles butt to the new dormer side walls (FIG. 3-13). Consult with a roofer or your roofing materials dealer for the proper methods and materials for the type of roof you're working with.

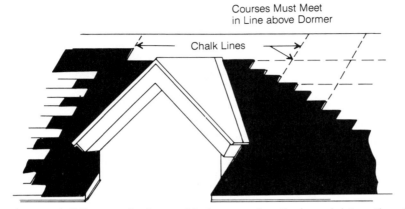

Courses Must Meet
in Line above Dormer

Chalk Lines

Fig. 3-11. *Use chalk lines to maintain even shingle courses above the dormer's intersection with the main roof.* (COURTESY OF CELOTEX CORPORATION)

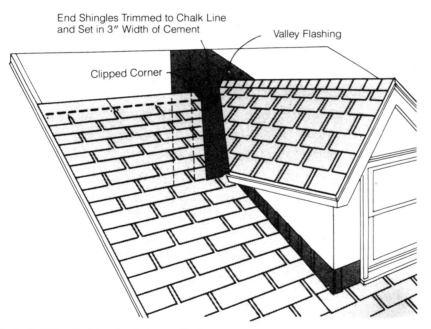

End Shingles Trimmed to Chalk Line
and Set in 3″ Width of Cement

Valley Flashing

Clipped Corner

Fig. 3-12. *Valley flashing details for a gable dormer.* (COURTESY OF CELOTEX CORPORATION)

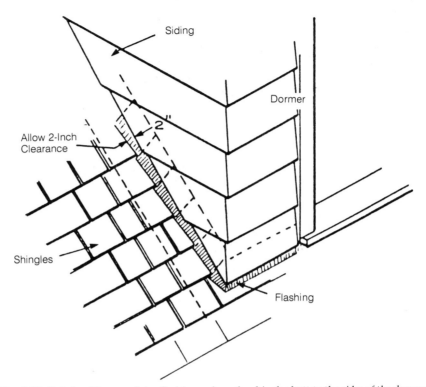

Siding

Dormer

Allow 2-Inch
Clearance

2"

Shingles

Flashing

Fig. 3-13. Details of the use of step flashings where the shingles butt to the sides of the dormer.

4
Skylights

NO MATTER WHAT THE AGE, SIZE, OR STYLE OF YOUR HOME, SKYLIGHTS CAN BE A welcome addition to your attic or garage remodeling project. Skylights can flood a room with natural light (FIG. 4-1) and can be used to brighten up the largest of areas or the smallest of dark corners. Operable skylights (FIG. 4-2) have the added advantage of providing supplementary ventilation that, when used in conjunction with your regular windows and doors, can help flush heat and stale odors out of the room in a hurry.

Thanks to the growing use of skylights in recent years, there is now a tremendous selection of types and sizes available. Many manufacturers now offer installation kits and good step-by-step instructions that really let you turn out a professional-quality job.

WHAT'S AVAILABLE

Before beginning your search for the perfect skylight, it helps to know what's available. There's a lot to choose from, so a little preplanning will help you select the skylight that's perfect for your needs.

Types of Skylights

There are two basic types of skylights: flat and domed. *Flat skylights* are made of tempered glass. Their flat configuration allows them to hug the roofline more closely and, therefore, be less obtrusive.

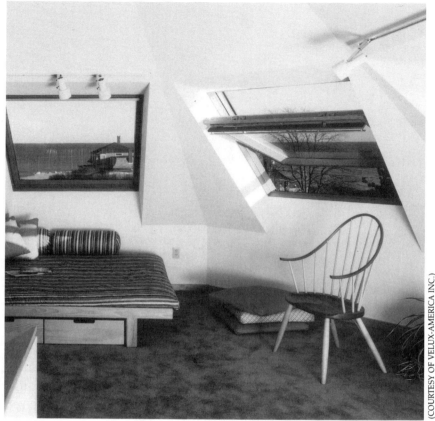

(COURTESY OF VELUX-AMERICA INC.)

Fig. 4-1. Operable skylights for natural light and ventilation in a remodeled attic.

Domed skylights are made from acrylic and are shaped something like a bubble. Their advantage is that the dome shape exposes more skylight area, allowing more light to enter the house. The dome protrudes up above the roofline rather noticeably, however, a look that not everyone likes. Also, acrylic is more prone to scratching than glass is, and some of the less expensive models are susceptible to leakage.

Both flat and dome skylights are available in double-pane models—an important energy-saving feature. Also, both types can be purchased with factory-applied tinting to minimize summer heat gain. (Glass skylights can also be tinted after installation, but acrylic can't.)

Frame Material

Skylight frames are usually made of either wood or aluminum. Wood frames, while more expensive, do not conduct heat as rapidly as metal and

(COURTESY OF VELUX-AMERICA INC.)

Fig. 4-2. A single large skylight helps make this attic bathroom bright and cheerful, while still offering maximum privacy.

are, therefore, more energy efficient. Also, depending on how much of the frame is visible inside, the wood gives you a warmer, more desirable appearance.

Metal frames are typically dark bronze in color, allowing them to blend in with almost any architectural style. Aluminum never needs painting and will hold up for many years without any maintenance. Aluminum frames are colder and more prone to icing than wood, however. This disadvantage can be overcome by purchasing a frame that is *thermally-broken*, meaning a small piece of vinyl or other low-conductance material separates the inner and outer halves of the frame, which minimizes the transference of cold through the metal.

Wood-frame skylights that are clad on the outside with aluminum offer the best of both worlds. While the most expensive of all the frame types, they offer the attractiveness of real wood on the inside with the durability and low maintenance of aluminum on the outside.

Operation

Skylights can be fixed or operable. Fixed skylights are for light only and do not open, while operable skylights (FIGS. 4-3 and 4-4) can be opened several

Fig. 4-3. A typical latch and pole arrangement for opening and closing an operable skylight.

Fig. 4-4. A sliding screen arrangement for an operable skylight.

inches to provide additional ventilation. This option, while adding to the initial cost, is well worth considering if the skylight is being placed where heat buildup is a problem, as in an attic. Some also have latches that permit the skylight to pivot to a vertical position (FIG. 4-5), allowing you to clean both sides of the glass from inside the house.

(COURTESY OF VELUX-AMERICA INC.)

Fig. 4-5. For ease of cleaning, this roof window pivots on special tracks to allow both sides to be reached from inside.

Size

There is a skylight size to fit into just about any space, and skylights can also be grouped together to fit larger areas. Most skylights are square or rectangular, and the greatest selection of sizes are in these two basic shapes. You can also find ovals, triangles, and a variety of other shapes to fit special needs, or you can have one custom made to your specifications.

All manufacturers offer a selection of 24-inch-wide skylights that fit between the roof rafters without any cutting and reframing. This is especially important if your home was constructed with roof trusses, which cannot be cut.

Optional Accessories

There are a variety of interesting optional accessories available, including:

Sliding shades (FIG. 4-6) mount in tracks below the skylight, allowing you to shade the glass. Several types are available, including translucent and

(COURTESY OF ANDERSEN WINDOWS)

Fig. 4-6. Light-controlling accordion shades over an operable skylight is an option available from the manufacturer.

opaque shades in various colors, and blackout shades for daytime sleepers.

Miniblinds, like those used over windows, can be used over skylights to adjust and filter the incoming light.

Electric motors can make operable skylights that will raise and lower the skylight from anywhere in the house.

Rain sensors can be attached to a skylight's electric motor. If rain is detected, the sensor will automatically trigger the motor to close the skylight.

Special flashings are available for installing a skylight on a flat roof or on heavy roofing materials such as tile. *Gang flashings,* which simplify connecting two or more skylights, are also available from most manufacturers.

INSTALLING SKYLIGHTS

Skylight installation is not a particularly difficult operation, although it does require some planning and some careful finish work. Also remember that, at least for part of the operation, you will be working on the roof, so observe all normal safety precautions.

If your home has a sloped ceiling, in which the ceiling is also the underside of the roof, then the skylight can simply be cut directly into the roof and the ceiling (FIG. 4-7). If you have a flat ceiling with an attic space between the top of the ceiling and the underside of the roof, you will need to construct a shaft to connect the two, allowing the light to be channeled from outside into the room below.

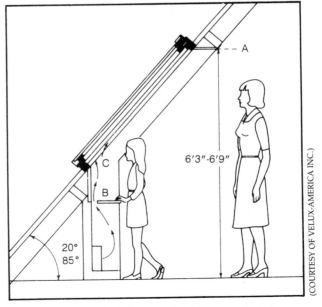

Fig. 4-7. Standard placement height for a roof window.

(COURTESY OF VELUX-AMERICA INC.)

One word of caution. If your roof was originally constructed using trusses, remember that the trusses *cannot* be cut in any way to accommodate the new skylight. There are several skylights on the market in both the fixed and operable varieties that will fit between the trusses, so you'll simply need to select one of these models.

SLOPED CEILINGS

First, select the type and size of skylight most appropriate to your needs, your budget, and the particular job site conditions. If possible, select one that will fit the space between the rafters without cutting in order to simplify the installation.

Next, locate where the skylight will sit on the roof, based on where you want it to open into the room below. The manufacturer will provide you with the exact rough opening size for the skylight you're using. Mark out the opening on the ceiling, then drive a nail or long drill bit up through the roof in each corner to transfer the exact location to the roof. If a rafter falls within the opening you've laid out, try and shift the opening to one side or the other to avoid additional cutting.

Preparing an Opening

If the skylight you're using is larger than the space between the rafters, or if rafter falls in the opening and the skylight can't be shifted to avoid it, the rafter will need to be cut out and removed. You will usually find it easiest to do this operation from inside the house, opening up a large enough section of the drywall or other ceiling finish material to expose the rafters. This minimizes the size of the hole that needs to be opened in the roof as well as the number of shingles that have to be patched back in.

First, mark the location and length of the rough opening on the rafter to be cut, then measure up and down the rafter an additional $1^1/2$ inches to allow for the framing lumber. Square cut the rafter at these two points, then remove and discard the cut section.

Using lumber that is the same size as the rafters, cut two pieces that will fit between the adjacent rafters on either side of the cut. Install the new pieces, nailing them to the two side rafters and into the ends of the cut rafters. Use a framing square to ensure that the opening remains square. Finally, install two more pieces of lumber to create the proper rough opening width, then mark the corners on the roof as described previously.

Installing the Skylight

Carefully remove the shingles about 12 inches beyond the marked opening in each direction. If possible, save the shingles for later use when patching in. Use a chalk line to mark the roof between the corner holes you created earlier, then cut through the roof sheathing to create the opening.

Depending on the type and manufacturer of the skylight, there are two basic installation procedures. One uses metal brackets to attach the skylight frame to the roof, the other requires the construction of a curb.

If your skylight is to be installed with the manufacturer's brackets (FIG. 4-8), the installation is somewhat simplified. Carefully following the installation instructions packed with the skylight, simply attach the brackets to the frame, center the skylight over the opening, and attach the brackets to the roof.

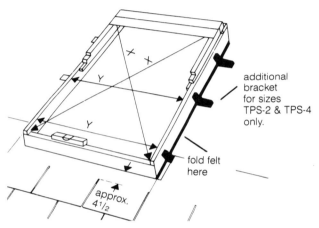

Fig. 4-8. Using a factory-supplied mounting bracket arrangement to simplify the attachment of the skylight to the roof. Letters indicate the manufacturer's dimensions for checking the rough opening to assure that the frame remains square. (COURTESY OF VELUX-AMERICA INC.)

If the skylight requires a *curb* (FIG. 4-9)—a simple box that raises the skylight above the roof—you will need to make this first. Curbs are usually constructed from four pieces of 2-×-6 lumber, nailed or screwed together into a frame of the correct dimensions for the skylight you're using. Follow the manufacturer's instructions for proper size and framing materials, then install the curb on the roof by toenailing it down to the rafters.

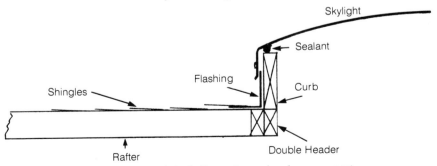

Fig. 4-9. A typical site-built opening and curb arrangement.

Flashings

The flashings that protect the curb or skylight frame from leaking are installed next. If possible, purchase a flashing kit directly from the manufacturer. It will contain all the pieces you need to complete the installation, and it will be correctly sized for the skylight you're using. If a kit is not available, you will need to have the proper flashings made up at a sheet-metal shop according to the manufacturer's instructions. Either way, you will need a bottom flashing, a top flashing, and several pieces of step flashing (FIG. 4-10).

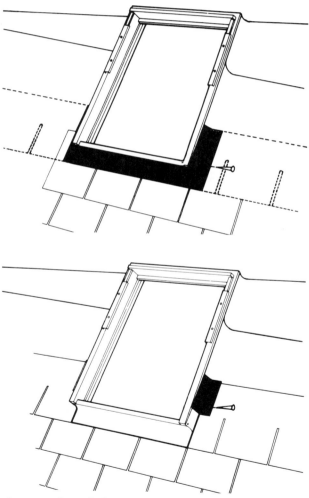

Fig. 4-10. *Top, bottom, and step flashings used with a skylight frame. This is an example of a manufacturer-supplied flashing kit, which greatly simplifies the installation.* (COURTESY OF VELUX-AMERICA INC.)

Fig. 4-10. Cont. (COURTESY OF VELUX-AMERICA INC.)

Install the flashings from the lower slope of the roof up to correctly overlap or underlap the shingles for complete weathertightness. Remember as you go that each shingle or piece of flashing must overlap the one *below* it (FIG. 4-11) so that water running down the roof cannot at any point work its way under the shingles and cause a leak.

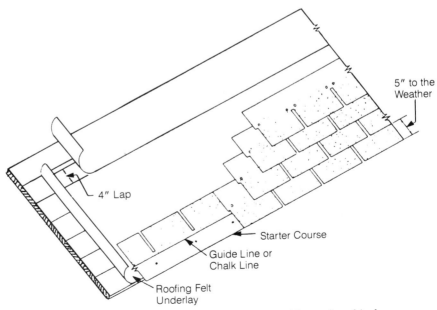

Fig. 4-11. Standard shingles techniques for three-tab composition roofing shingles.

Begin by replacing the shingles up to the low side of the skylight frame or curb (FIG. 4-12), then install the bottom flashing so that it overlaps those shingles. Continue working your way up the roof. Patch each course of shingles up to the sides of the skylight and install a piece of step flashing at the end of each course, interwoven with the shingles (FIG. 4-13). When you reach the top of the skylight, install the top flashing, then patch the upper rows of shingles in over it.

Fig. 4-12. *Patching new shakes in around two new fixed skylights. Note the installation brackets near the bottom of each skylight.*

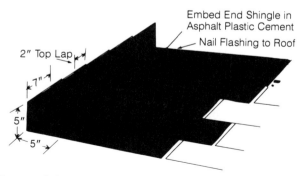

Fig. 4-13. *Using step flashings where the shingles meet the skylight.* (COURTESY OF CELOTEX CORPORATION)

The last step is the installation of the skylight itself. How this is done will vary from manufacturer to manufacturer. Some types have installation brackets or tracks that hold the skylight to the frame. Other types simply overlap the curb and are installed with screws over a bed of sealant. Follow the manufacturer's recommendations carefully and install the skylight exactly as they instruct. Finally, use drywall, wood, or other material as desired to finish off the inside of the opening.

FLAT CEILINGS

If your home has an attic space between the roof and the ceiling, then a shaft will be necessary to get the light from the roof to the rooms below. Skylight shafts are relatively easy to construct, and they offer several advantages. For one, the bottom of the shaft can be made larger than the top, allowing a large opening in the ceiling while using a smaller, less expensive skylight. A shaft can also be used to offset the ceiling opening to the roof opening, allowing you to place the skylight between the rafters without additional roof framing while still maintaining an opening that is centered in the room below.

Shafts take three basic forms, depending on your needs and particular installation conditions (FIG. 4-14):

Straight shafts are framed straight up from the ceiling, at a right angle to the ceiling joists. They are the easiest to construct but, being offset to the roof, allow the least amount of light.

Angled shafts are at a right angle to the pitch of the roof, rather than to the ceiling. The angled cuts make these shafts a little harder to build, but because the shaft comes straight in off the skylight, more light is admitted.

Splayed shafts have a ceiling opening that is larger than the actual skylight (FIGS. 4-15 and 4-16), either in width, length, or both. They can be adjusted to center the opening to the room. This is the hardest type of shaft to construct, but admits the most light.

Constructing the Shaft

First, lay out and mark the desired opening on the ceiling. This opening can be adjusted in virtually any way you wish—you can center it in the room, you can make it square or rectangular, or you can move it to miss joists or other obstructions.

Next, lay out the skylight's position. Center the roof opening to the ceiling opening as much as possible to simplify the framing of the shaft. Refer to the manufacturer's instructions for the proper rough opening size, then cut out and frame the roof opening as directed previously. Install the skylight and flashings, and patch in the shingles.

Cut back the ceiling drywall along the lines of the opening you laid out. Following the procedures outlined previously, cut and box the ceiling joists

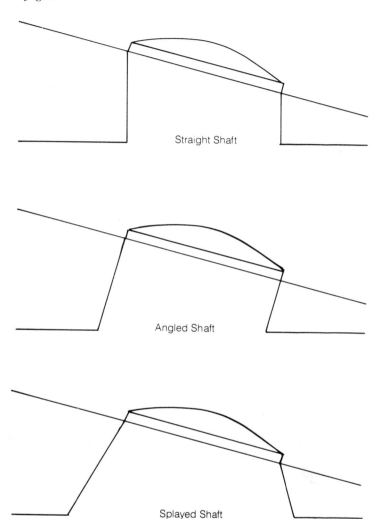

Straight Shaft

Angled Shaft

Splayed Shaft

Fig. 4-14. Typical light shaft configurations. The splayed shaft (bottom) allows a ceiling opening that is larger than the skylight itself.

to frame the opening in the ceiling. If your opening is over 6 feet in either direction, double the joists and cross joists.

Constructing the shaft is merely a matter of connecting the roof opening with the ceiling opening. Use 2-×-4 lumber, cut to the proper lengths and angles, and install the walls of the shaft on 24-inch centers. Finally, cover over the framing with drywall on the inside of the shaft, and tape and top the seams to achieve a smooth finish. On the attic side, install R-19 insulation to minimize heat loss through the shaft into the attic. A coat of semigloss white paint will help reflect more light down the shaft.

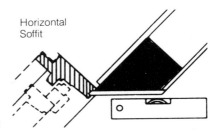

Horizontal
Soffit

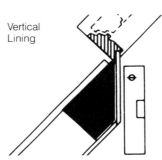

Vertical
Lining

Fig. 4-15. Framing the skylight opening to create a horizontal line at the top and a vertical line at the bottom. (COURTESY OF VELUX-AMERICA INC.)

Fig. 4-16. A small splayed shaft that has been drywalled to match the surrounding ceiling.

5
Framing
the Basement

BASEMENT RENOVATIONS PRESENT A DIFFERENT SET OF REMODELING SITUATIONS than an attic does, and in many ways they are less complicated. Assuming a structurally solid floor and exterior walls, the typical basement remodeling requires primarily cosmetic work to get it ready for occupancy.

The biggest problems usually encountered in a basement are dampness, lack of insulation, and a maze of pipes, wires, and other unsightly obstacles that need to be relocated and concealed. In some basements, where no thought was given to esthetics when it was originally constructed, the initial room you're presented with might seem a little overwhelming! But just take it one step at a time, dealing with each situation as it arises, and in no time at all you'll have a basement you can be really proud of.

PLANNING

During the initial planning stages in chapter 1, you evaluated your needs and laid out a plan for the basement's use, whether it's to be a family room, office, hobby room, or whatever. Now is a good time to study the basement in a little more detail and refine those plans as necessary.

As with the attic, your first concern is head room. Once again, the $7^1/2$-foot code for finished ceiling height will apply, but the building inspectors will usually grant you a little more leeway here. They realize that little if anything can be done to change the height of the ceiling in an existing basement, so if you can't quite make the ceiling height requirements, ask what they will allow.

When figuring your finished ceiling height, remember that you need to allow for the ceiling material you'll be using. If your situation is such that you can install drywall directly onto the underside of the floor joists, then the allowance is minimal—just 1/2 or 5/8 inch. If, as often happens in basements, pipes or ducts protrude below the floor joists, then you might need to install a suspended ceiling, which will hang a minimum of about 2 inches below the joists to allow for installation of the tracks and panels. See chapter 9 for complete drywall and suspended ceiling installation details.

If the obstacles you encounter on the ceiling are isolated in one or two spots—a plumbing trap or a section of heat duct for example—you can probably just box those areas in and cover over them without adversely affecting the ceiling height in the rest of the room.

Other things will affect your initial planning. What is the condition of the floor? Will it need to be furred up to level it and cover any cracks or other irregularities? Will the exterior walls need to be furred out for insulation or to avoid obstacles? The amount of space used up by the furring can often be 1/2 foot or more and needs to be considered early on if you hope to achieve rooms of certain dimensions.

If you haven't already done so, make a scale drawing of the basement. Show major obstacles and how you will cover them. Indicate those walls that will be furred out and by how much. This will make it much easier to accurately lay out any interior partitions.

Finally, look at your plumbing and wiring needs. If you intend to install a bathroom, its location might be limited by the availability of existing waste lines. Electrical wiring is usually more flexible, but there still might be factors that limit where some of your wiring might be placed.

CORRECTING MOISTURE PROBLEMS

Before you begin the renovation work in the basement, you must correct any existing moisture problems. It is very important that you take the time and care to fix these problems correctly at this stage of the remodeling, before they adversely affect the finished basement.

There are two basic causes of moisture problems in the basement: *seepage* of rainwater from the outside and *condensation* from interior sources. Each has different causes and different cures.

Seepage

Seepage problems occur when rainwater from around the outside of your hosue works its way into the basement. This rainwater seepage can occur at a variety of locations and might take a little time and patience to track down and correct properly.

General Seepage—an overall "damp" feeling to the basement—can usually be corrected by taking simple steps to route the rainwater away from the house. Take these measures first because they might cure the problem without resorting to more involved and expensive solutions. Here are some things to look for:

Grade Level. Check the level and slope of the ground around the foundation (FIG. 5-1). The dirt should have a definite grade away from the house so that water will not drain back against the foundation. Correct any slope problems you encounter by grading the earth to the proper slope or by adding additional earth against the foundation. Maintain a minimum of 6 inches of clearance between the top of the dirt and the bottom of the siding or other wood.

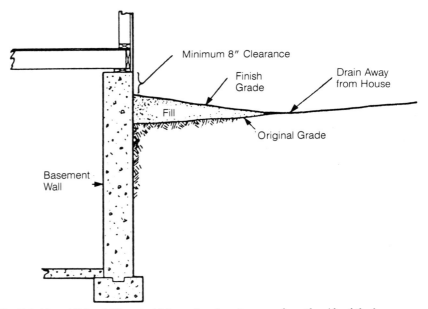

Fig. 5-1. Use additional fill material to grade rainwater away from the side of the house.

Also, check the area between the house and any sidewalks or driveways. If the concrete of the sidewalk is substantially higher than the dirt, it can act as a dam to trap water against the house.

Pipes and Sprinklers. Be certain that exterior faucets do not leak and that there are no leaks in any of the pipes around the outside of the house. Pay particular attention to the main shutoff valve where it enters the house and to any sprinkler system pipes that are buried around the perimeter.

Gutters and Downspouts (FIG. 5-2). Rain gutters at the eaves of the roof should be in good condition and free of any leaks. Thoroughly clean out the gutters to remove leaves, pine needles, dirt, or other debris. Use a garden hose to fill the gutters and check for leaks around all the seams and fastener

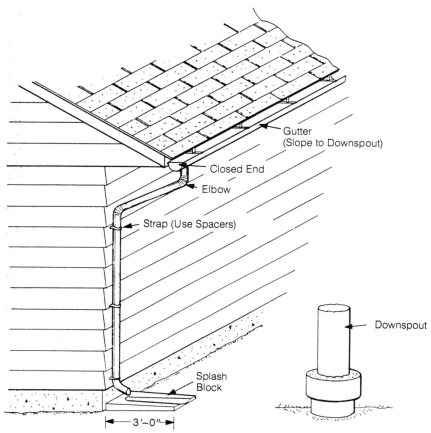

Fig. 5-2. *A 3-foot splash block at the end of a downspout might not be sufficient for draining runoff away from the house. The downspout adaptor (right) ties a downspout into an underground pipe leading to a dry well.*

penetrations. Correct any leaks with a good grade of roof sealant. If you are missing sections of gutter, or if your home does not currently have any, install new pieces to complete the system around the entire house. Downspouts should also be in good repair and completely free of any obstructions or leaks.

One of the most common drainage and seepage problems occurs when water from the gutters and downspouts is allowed to accumulate around the foundation. Most people use a simple splash block under the end of the downspout, though in many cases this is not sufficient to channel the water away from the house. At the very least, put an extender on the bottom of the downspout that is long enough to channel the water well away from the foundation and over to an area where the natural slope of the ground will carry it away from the house. Do this for each downspout.

Installing a Dry Well. A better solution is to install a *dry well* (FIG. 5-3). Dry wells receive the runoff from the gutters and allow it to seep back into the ground a safe distance away from the house.

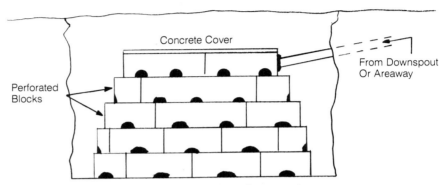

Fig. 5-3. Typical dry well construction.

To construct a dry well, simply excavate a 5-foot deep, 5-foot diameter hole in the ground about 10 to 12 feet away from the house. Line the inside of the hole with *cesspool blocks* (perforated concrete blocks) arranged in a circle. Arrange the first course with approximately nine blocks, then stack an eight-block circle of slightly smaller diameter on that. Follow this with four more circles of eight, seven, six, and five blocks respectively. The blocks are simply stacked in place, holes down, with no mortar.

At the fifth course up from the bottom, insert a section of 4-inch plastic pipe into the block course and mortar it into place. Route this pipe to the downspout, making certain it is angled to flow from the downspout to the well. Cap the dry well with a concrete cover, then backfill around the blocks. Use a downspout adaptor to connect the bottom of the downspout to the end of the 4-inch pipe.

A well this size should handle the runoff from one or two downspouts or areaways (FIG. 5-4). Place additional wells as needed, depending on the number of downspouts you have and the extent of the seepage problem you're encountering.

Isolated Seepage. First of all, study the existing conditions and look for clues to the location of the seepage. Moisture might be coming up through cracks in the concrete of the basement walls or through loose or missing grout joints between concrete blocks. It might also be from cracks in the floor or around wall and floor penetrations.

Obvious, isolated areas of seepage, such as a broken grout joint, are the first things to repair. There are a variety of patching and sealing compounds on the market for this task. (Consult with your building materials dealer for the correct product for your situation.)

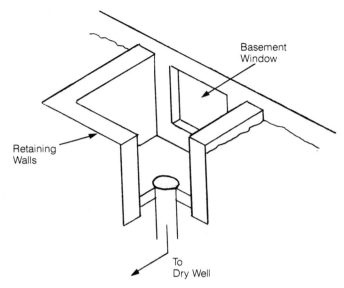

Fig. 5-4. *An areaway outside a basement window shows the central drain leading to the dry well. Areaways can also be enlarged, terraced, and landscaped, offering a better rainwater absorption and a more pleasant view out the window.*

If seepage persists after you have repaired the obvious, isolated leaks, and if you have also made every effort to channel rainwater away from the house, then your basement might require the installation of exterior footing drains (FIG. 5-5) or basement wall waterproofing (FIG. 5-6). Both of these mea-

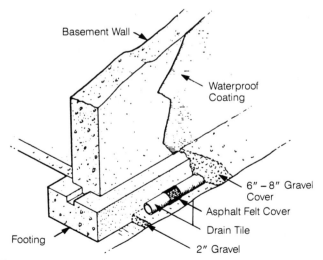

Fig. 5-5. *An example of a footing drain at the bottom of a basement wall.*

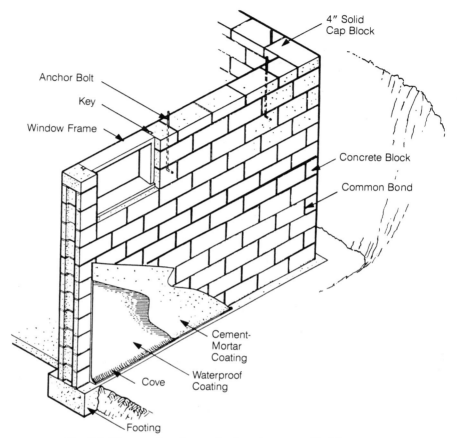

Fig. 5-6. *Waterproofing the exterior face of a concrete block basement.*

sures require a considerable amount of excavating around the perimeter of the house—all the way down to the footings. As such, they are best left to a professional contractor with experience in these kinds of situations.

Condensation

The other main cause of basement dampness is condensation. Water vapor is generated in the home in a number of ways, including cooking, washing, houseplants, and—the biggest source of all—breathing. This moisture vapor remains in suspension in the warm air of the house until it meets a cold surface, at which point it condenses and turns back into visible water.

Basements, because of their colder surface temperatures and lack of good ventilation, are a natural spot for this condensation to occur. Condensation leads to a damp, musty feeling in the air and, in more extreme cases, the actual formation of mildew and mold.

There are two relatively simple solutions to condensation problems—heat and ventilation. Adding one or two ducts off the existing heating system or installing electric room heaters in the walls (FIGS. 5-7 and 5-8) will greatly help the problem. Insulation added to the walls will keep these surfaces warmer, so the moisture will not condense as readily, and will also make the heating system work more efficiently.

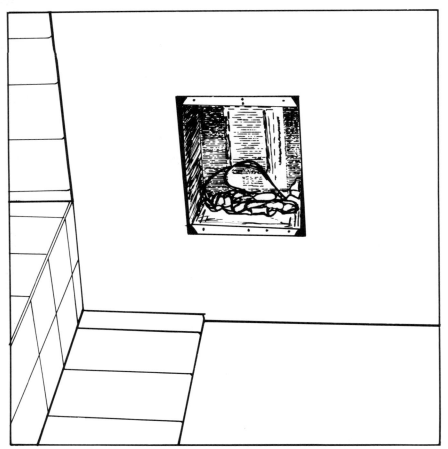

Fig. 5-7. The rough-in can and wiring for a small electric wall heater.

Add operable windows wherever possible to increase the cross flow of air. Also add ventilation fans to remove moisture-laden air from the room, especially in laundry and bathroom areas. Remember that ventilation fans must be ducted all the way to the outside, otherwise you are just taking the damaging moisture from one area of the house and moving it to another. In more serious cases, you might wish to consider the installation of a dehumidifier.

(COURTESY OF NUTONE)

Fig. 5-8. An attractive, efficient, fan-forced electric heater. Note the individual thermostat on the face of the unit.

FURRING

The typical basement has concrete or concrete block walls, no insulation, and a number of exposed obstacles. To overcome these handicaps and achieve a warm, smoothly finished room, furring is used (FIG. 5-9). *Furring* is simply the act of placing new lumber on the walls, floor, and ceiling to create insulation cavities, to box in exposed pipes, and to level everything out to receive the finishing materials.

For most furring applications, 2-×-4 lumber works fine (FIG. 5-10). If the lumber will be in direct contact with concrete walls or will rest on the concrete floor, then those boards must be pressure-treated. This prevents moisture from wicking out from the concrete and rotting the wood.

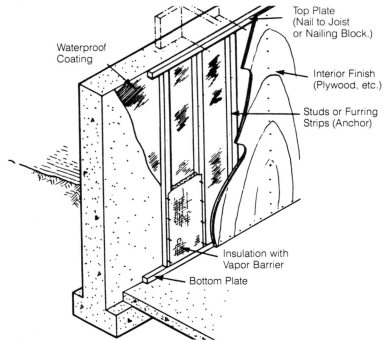

Fig. 5-9. Using 2-×-4 furring over the inside of a basement wall creates an insulation cavity and a straight base for the installation of the drywall.

Fig. 5-10. Furring over concrete block walls.

Depending on the material you'll be furring over, you can use a variety of fastening methods. Masonry nails work fine in concrete block and in newer, softer concrete. In old, hard concrete, you'll have a very hard time driving the nails and getting them to hold. Many rental yards rent powder-activated nailers (FIG. 5-11), which use a small gunpowder charge to drive a tempered steel nail through the wood and into the concrete. The pins and powder charges are a little expensive, but the nailers are fast and work very well in hard concrete and even some types of steel. Follow the manufacturer's instructions carefully for proper handling and safety precautions.

Fig. 5-11. Using a powder-activated gun to shoot a steel pin into a concrete block wall.

There are a variety of anchors that will work, including lag shields and expansion anchors. Installed properly, anchors give the strongest grip and are especially useful in attaching heavier lumber or in very irregular walls where a lot of shimming is necessary. Installing anchors is rather time consuming. You will need to use a rotary hammer and carbide bit to predrill the concrete to receive the anchor, then predrill each board for the bolts. Most anchors will not work in hollow concrete block, so check with your dealer when making your selection.

Construction adhesive works fine in most applications (be sure to use one rated for use with pressure-treated lumber), unless the wall is extremely uneven and you can't get a good bead of adhesive to contact the furring. You should also consider using adhesive along with whatever nails or other fasteners you're using to ensure a tighter, longer-lasting installation.

WALL FURRING

In most basements, furring out the walls is all you'll have to worry about. This is the area where you'll need the maximum insulation, and it's also the area that is usually the most roughly finished.

For most applications, 2-×-4 lumber placed on edge will work fine as furring (FIGS. 5-12 and 5-13). It is heavy enough to smooth out irregularities, it allows the installation of 1¹/₂-inch rigid insulation (see chapter 7), and it minimizes the amount of interior floor space that you lose.

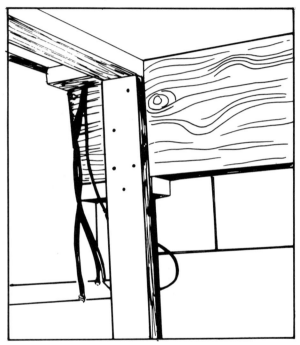

Fig. 5-12. *Furring details at a concrete block wall. Note the cable television wires behind the furring.*

Begin by laying a board horizontally at the bottom of the wall (FIG. 5-14). Attach the board to the wall, using one or more of the fastening options discussed previously. Shims might be necessary between the wall and the back of the board to fill in any low spots and to prevent the board from bowing in when fastened. After the bottom board is in and secured, do the same at the top of the wall.

Starting at one corner, mark the top and bottom boards on 24-inch centers. Cut 2-×-4 uprights to fit snugly between the boards, then fasten them in place. Be careful to maintain the 24-inch center spacing as this will simplify the installation of the finish wall covering.

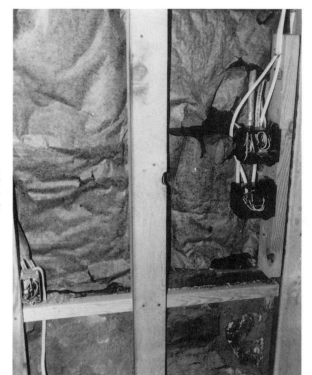

Fig. 5-13. Furring with 2-×-4 lumber over a stone wall. The furring also creates a space for running the electrical wires.

Fig. 5-14. Furring using 1-×-4 lumber over a 2-×-2 base.

If you encounter obstacles (FIG. 5-15), such as pipes or heating ducts, simply box around them. Lay a pressure-treated 2 × 4 on the floor, then use a level to mark the same location on the ceiling and install a second 2 × 4 there. Finally, install additional 2-×-4 uprights between the plates, toenailing them to the top and bottom boards.

Fig. 5-15. Notch furring to build out around a chimney.

PARTITION WALLS

It's a simple matter to install partition walls wherever you desire to divide up the interior space. The partitions are not load-bearing (FIG. 5-16), and they can be constructed with 2-×-4 lumber and standard framing practices (FIG. 5-17).

Mark the layout of the walls on the floor, then snap chalk lines to indicate where they will be placed. Use pressure-treated lumber laid flat for the sole plate and fasten it directly to the floor along the chalk lines. Use a plumb bob to transfer the location of the sole plate to the ceiling, snap another chalk line, then install the top plate by nailing it to the ceiling joists. If the wall is parallel to the joists and falls in between them, place blocking between the joists and secure the top plate to the blocking.

Use 2 × 4s on 16-inch centers for the studs, cutting each one to length as you go (in case the floor slopes). Toenail the studs to the top and bottom plates using 8d nails. Use a standard trimmer/header arrangement over any door openings.

A garage conversion offers the ideal spot for a new exercise area. This one is spacious, warm, and fully carpeted for comfort, with a built-in spa set neatly into one corner. The post, which had to remain for structural reasons, was turned into an asset with the addition of custom-made towel hooks.

Remodeling opportunities abound for creating a basement home office space that's perfect for your needs. The use of a suspended ceiling grid and prefinished wall panels speeds and simplifies the remodeling.

Space was borrowed from the garage to enlarge this kitchen and provide a new dining area. A new hardwood floor and extensive solid-wood mouldings beautifully complement the decor.

The entire gable end wall of this attic was replaced with glass, maximizing the spectacular view. Two operable skylights provide additional natural light and help to ventilate the room. Notice the special framing, behind the bed, that provides a tall area for the headboard and lower areas for storage cabinets and counter spaces.

A low kneewall, built out slightly from the wall and capped with a narrow shelf, offers a place for furniture, a baseboard heater, and a sunny spot for plants. The stained beams add a beautiful, decorative highlight. Note the large, pivoting roof windows used for ventilation and lots of natural light.

Velux-America Inc.

This small attic conversion makes for a perfect extra bedroom. The pivoting roof windows provide light and ventilation, as does the window in the gable wall at the end of the room.

Georgia-Pacific

A spacious family and entertainment room was created when this attic was converted to living space. Kneewalls were placed at a convenient height for the bookcases. Light is provided by a combination of skylights and track-lighting. The ceiling extends all the way to the old ridge, without the use of ceiling joists, giving the room more height.

A small sink area can be tucked into an alcove in virtually any attic, basement, or garage conversion. Wall-mounted cabinets with tambour doors are used to create both storage and counter space in one compact arrangement.

In this beautiful renovation, attic space was converted to a new bathroom that is complete with a stall shower, double sinks, and a large roof window. Note the clear cedar strips on the ceiling, the recessed lighting, and the large mirror that helps keep the room feeling spacious.

A small but stylish bathroom was tucked into this basement when it was remodeled. All the amenities are grouped in a comfortable arrangement and nicely tied together with the extensive use of ceramic tile. Note the small basement window that was incorporated into the wall of the shower.

Using a platform can often ease potential plumbing problems in a basement or garage installation. The platform is not only convenient and visually pleasing, it also helps create the necessary slope for the plumbing.

A little imagination and a few sheets of plywood can make a new guest bedroom into a practical, efficient space—with abundant storage possibilities.

A colorful bedroom with abundant built-in work and storage areas can take the place of a seldom-used garage. Even the bed is handmade!

A bank of roof windows does wonders to brighten up this attic space. Kneewalls were not used, the existing rafters were covered with natural lumber, and the large support timbers and struts were left exposed and painted white. Note the use of a partition wall at the left to create a small bathroom space at the end of the room.

This perfectly converted basement offers every family room amenity imaginable. There are spacious conversation and reading areas, a fully equipped bar (complete with wine racks), and a small bumper pool table, bookcase, and game-storage cabinets. The 2-×-4-foot suspended ceiling panels simplify the concealing of the framing and plumbing above the room, and the mouldings add warmth and color.

Fig. 5-16. Interior, nonbearing partition walls create a corner bathroom.

PLUMBING AND ELECTRICAL WIRING

After the walls are furred and the partition walls are in place, install any plumbing and electrical wiring. If there is little in the way of existing wiring in the basement, you will need to extend new circuits into the area from the service panel. Plan on one 15-amp light and plug circuit for each 500 square feet of floor area, plus any dedicated circuits that are required for large appliances or tools. Consult with your building department for the exact requirements for your situation.

Plumbing in the basement can be tricky because it is often below the level of the existing sewer lines. If you cannot tie into an existing sewer pipe and maintain the required slope of ¹/₄ inch per foot of run, you will need to install a sewage pump to pump the waste up to the level of the existing pipes. Upflush toilets are also available, which use jets of high-pressure water to break up solid waste and force it up to the sewer lines. Check with an experienced plumber to determine the right equipment for your basement.

FLOORS AND FLOORING

Take a look at the condition of the existing floor and determine what methods and materials you will be using to finish it. Typically, the existing floor will be a concrete slab, often sloped to a floor drain somewhere near the cen-

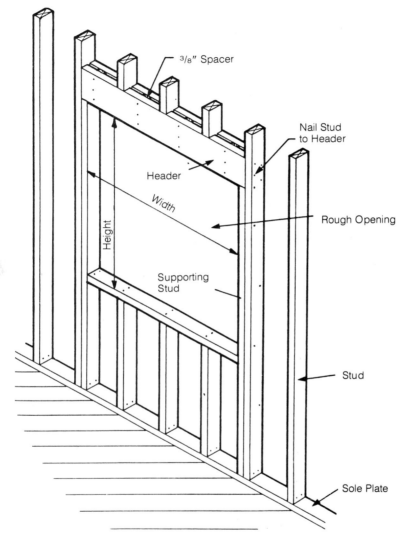

3/8" Spacer

Nail Stud
to Header

Header

Width

Rough Opening

Height

Supporting
Stud

Stud

Sole Plate

Fig. 5-17. Standard framing details for bearing or nonbearing walls.

ter of the room. If the floor is relatively smooth, level, and free of large cracks, you can probably install your finish flooring directly over it. If the floor is in poor condition, or if it's damp from condensation, fur it over.

Furring the Floor

Furring the floor consists of anchoring pressure-treated 2-×-4 lumber, called *sleeps*, directly to the slab to create a new base for the floor covering. A *vapor barrier*—a layer of 6-mil plastic sheeting designed to prevent ground moisture from coming up through the slab into the house—should also be incorporated with the furring at the same time.

The vapor barrier can be installed directly on the floor by placing it on a thin layer of mastic or draping it over the sleepers (FIG. 5-18). Lay the sleepers flat on 16-inch centers—snapping chalk lines on the floor will simplify the layout—and anchor them to the concrete with one of the fastening methods described previously. You might need to use shims to keep the sleepers level on badly cracked or sloped slabs. If you need to raise the height of the floor in order to clear obstacles, the 2-×-4 sleepers can be laid on edge, or you can use 2-×-6 or 2-×-8 lumber on edge.

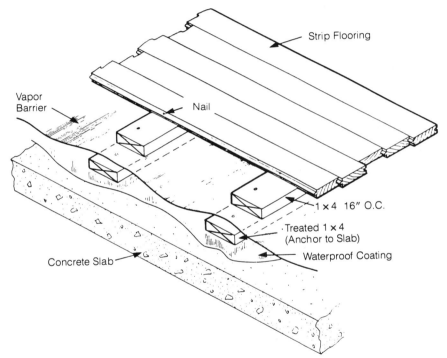

Fig. 5-18. Installing a vapor barrier and furring over a concrete basement floor.

If you are installing a tongue-and-groove hardwood floor, install the flooring strips directly over the sleepers. For carpeting, linoleum, or other floor covering materials, first install a subfloor of 5/8-inch or 3/4-inch tongue-and-groove plywood, nailed to the sleepers.

Floors with Furring

If the floor is not being furred, the use of a vapor barrier is still an important consideration. If the basement slab is relatively new, the building codes will have required the installation of a vapor barrier underneath the concrete when it was poured. Basements in older homes were rarely built with a vapor barrier, so you will need to plan on installing one when you lay the flooring. If you have any doubts about whether your basement floor has an existing vapor barrier, don't take any chances—go ahead and install a new one with the flooring.

Linoleum or Floor Tiles

If you are putting down linoleum over the existing concrete, using a waterproof adhesive will create an adequate vapor barrier. The same is true for ceramic tile, most types of vinyl and rubber floor tiles, and most types of glue-down carpeting. Consult with your floor covering supplier for the correct adhesive for your application. Use a patching compound intended for floors to patch any cracks and low spots. Seal the concrete with a primer, if necessary, then spread the mastic and apply the flooring.

Wall-to-Wall Carpeting

Plan on installing a vapor barrier under wall-to-wall carpeting because the carpet and pad alone are not sufficient to do the job. Use 6-mil plastic sheeting laid directly on the floor and overlap it 12 inches at the seams and a few inches up the walls (the drywall or baseboard will cover it). Use roofing mastic or other sealant to seal the seams and edges along the wall. The tack strip, pad, and carpet can then be laid over the vapor barrier.

6
Converting Garages

CONVERTING A GARAGE INTO USABLE LIVING SPACE IS TYPICALLY THE EASIEST AND most straightforward of all three of the remodeling projects. The average garage already has a good, usable floor; solid, above-grade walls that are already sided to match the house; plenty of head room; and a weathertight roof. In addition, there is usually very little to worry about in the way of exposed plumbing, heating ducts, mechanical equipment, or other obstacles.

Probably the most difficult task you'll face will be the removal of the garage doors and the subsequent patching in of the openings. Care must be exercised in safely handling the heavy doors and hardware, and you'll want to take the time to carefully plan out how you'll fill in the old door areas to match and blend with the surrounding house.

SOME OPTIONS FOR THE OPENINGS

First and foremost, your goal here is to fill in the old garage door openings in such a manner that it will not be immediately obvious that this was once a garage. With a little thought and patience, this is not as difficult as it might at first seem.

For starters, you'll want to consider just what you'd like to do with those openings. After all, removing a double-car garage door leaves a 16-foot-×-7-foot hole and removing a single-car garage door leaves a 8- or 9-foot-×-7-foot hole—pretty good size holes in the wall!

Filling in the openings with windows (FIG. 6-1) or sliding glass doors (FIG. 6-2) is an obvious first choice, and a good one in most circumstances. But

(COURTESY OF ANDERSEN WINDOWS)

Fig. 6-1. An example of good-quality windows. Note the nailing flange around the outside for attaching the window to the framing.

before you make that decision, look at these massive openings from within the framework of your overall plan for the remodeling. What are your plans for the garage? Will it become a game room? Bedroom? Hobby room? Dark room? An extension of the existing living room or kitchen?

Fig. 6-2. A typical sliding glass door.

With that in mind, determine where those openings will fall in relation to the intended rooms. If, for example, part of the garage will be converted into a new kitchen, you might need to partially or completely close off the openings to provide the necessary wall space for cabinets. On the other hand, for a game room or an art studio, filling in the openings with windows will provide lots of natural light for the pool table or the easel.

You'll also want to look at where the openings are in relation to what's outside the garage. If the openings face the street in front, as many do, you might not want to install large sliding glass doors because the resulting noise and lack of privacy would make them impractical. If, however, they open onto the side of the house where it's relatively peaceful, perhaps that area could be fenced off to make a private garden. The openings could be filled with windows or French doors to create a beautiful new study or master bedroom suite.

Remember, too, that you are not stuck with the location of those openings. The typical garage represents a pretty large area with a considerable amount of wall space. There's nothing to prevent you from simply closing off the old openings completely and creating new window and door areas elsewhere (FIG. 6-3).

As in the example of the garage doors that face the busy, noisy front street, you might consider installing new framing in the openings. Packing the wall cavities with insulation will limit the noise and heat loss. Then you can install solid siding in front to match the rest of the house, perhaps with one or two small windows for architectural interest. Select a quiet area to the rear of the garage, or a wall with a nice view, and install new windows there.

DRIVEWAYS

One of the most common mistakes that people make when converting a garage into living space is to ignore the old driveway. No matter how much care and planning went into restructuring the front of the garage to match the existing house, nothing calls more attention to your conversion than a concrete driveway leading directly up to a solid wall! This not only detracts from the aesthetics of the front of your house, it lowers the resale value of the work you've done.

During the planning stages, give some serious thought to redesigning the driveway so that it blends in with the overall remodeling scheme, or perhaps consider removing it all together. Here are some examples:

□ If you plan to place a carport in front of the existing garage, the driveway could serve that structure without looking out of place.

□ If the garage is being converted into a family room with a door to the outside onto the old driveway, you could leave part of the concrete in place to make a basketball area or other outdoor activity spot. Remove part of the driveway where it connects to the street, then the portion that remains will look as though it was meant to be there.

□ If you wish to remove part of the driveway at the street, you could then cover what remains with a wood deck. This will blend in perfectly if you fill in the garage door opening with a French or sliding glass door. The door will simply open out onto a deck.

□ If you intend to close off the old openings completely, or if you can't blend the front of the garage into the driveway in any other manner, give some serious thought to removing the driveway altogether. You can break it up by hand and haul it off a little at a time, or have a contractor come in and remove it. You can then patch in the yard with new lawn or other plantings, and the converted garage will blend in much more readily. For a truly finished appearance, have the curb in front of the house rebuilt to eliminate the depression where the driveway used to join the street.

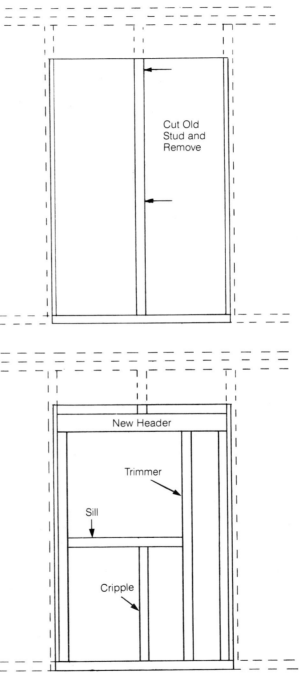

Fig. 6-3. Cutting and framing procedure for creating a new window opening.

PASSIVE SOLAR

If your garage door openings face south, you might use this area to gain some free heat from the sun. There are two primary considerations that go into creating a passive solar sunspace—glazing and mass.

Glazing

Glazing is simply the glass that allows the sunlight to enter the room. For a sunspace, the glazing area should equal approximately 10 to 15 percent of the room's floor area. For example, a 20-foot-×-20-foot garage would have 400 square feet of floor area. Take 10 to 15 percent of 400, and you'll see that you need 40 to 60 square feet of glass, which can easily be incorporated into the large openings left when the garage doors are removed.

The glass should face as close to true south (not magnetic south) as possible to maximize the gain from the sun in the winter. If the glass is within 30 degrees of south in either direction (west or east of south), you'll still have about 85 to 90 percent of the possible sunlight available to you, and this will work fine. Also, the glass should be blocked as little as possible by trees, buildings, or other obstacles. Remember that deciduous trees loose their leaves in the winter and will not be as great an obstruction as they appear to be in the summer.

Mass

In order for a sunspace to work, the sunlight must be absorbed after it enters the house and held so that you can extract the heat from it. *Mass* is the term that is used for this heat-absorbing material.

The two simplest and most effective mass materials are masonry and water. Masonry mass could be concrete, brick, rock, or concrete block. It must be 4 to 6 inches thick, be directly exposed to the sunlight and have a surface area of approximately three times the glass area.

For example, if you have 50 square feet of glass, you'll need about 150 square feet of masonry, 4 to 6 inches thick. This is ideal for garages where the thick concrete slab floor is already in place and can act as the mass. If you don't wish to leave the bare concrete, cover it with a more attractive masonry material, such as brick or ceramic tile. Carpet or wood flooring will not allow the sunlight to penetrate to the mass and should not be used.

Water is usually a little more difficult to incorporate into the room. You can place water in clear plastic cylinders or in black-painted steel containers, again directly exposed to the sunlight. Plan on using about 3 gallons of water for every 1 square foot of south-facing glass.

REMOVING THE GARAGE DOORS

Removing the old garage doors is heavy, awkward, and if improperly done, dangerous work. Before beginning the removal of the doors, study their construction carefully. Have the proper tools and materials on hand, work slowly and carefully, and have a helper available. If you have any doubts about removing the doors, call an experienced contractor to do the job for you.

There are four basic types of garage doors: swinging, sliding, swing-up overhead, and roll-up overhead. Each is installed and removed a little differently. In addition, you might have an electric garage door opener to remove.

If you do not have a use for the doors or the opener after their removal, consider placing an ad in the newspaper and selling them. There's usually a good market for items such as these, especially if you're careful during the removal process and save all of the parts.

Electric Garage Door Openers

To remove an electric garage door opener, first unplug the motor unit or disconnect it from its electrical service. Next, unbolt the carrier from the garage door (FIG. 6-4), then unbolt the motor unit from its supports. With a helper, lower the motor unit to the ground, then unbolt the end of the motor track from the wall. Finally, remove the rest of the brackets from the door and the supports from the ceiling.

Swinging Doors

Swinging garage doors were common on older houses but are not seen that often anymore. Two doors meet in the middle of the opening and are mounted on hinges at each side. They open out on the hinges, swinging away to each side.

These are probably the easiest of all the door types to remove. First, place blocks under the doors so that they won't sag as you remove the hinges. Have a helper brace the door in the closed position, then remove the screws that hold the hinges to the door frame. With your helper, lower the door to the ground. Repeat for the other side, then remove and discard the old trim around the openings.

Sliding Doors

Sliding doors are more common in barns, but they are sometimes used on garages also. Two or more doors slide on an overhead track and either butt each other or overlap.

These doors are removed by disassembling the roller mechanisms that hold them in the overhead track. Block under the doors to take up the space

Fig. 6-4. The carrier arm of an electric garage door opener where it's attached to the door.

between the ground and the bottom of the door. Have a helper brace the door, then remove the screws that hold the roller bracket to the top of the door and lower the door to the ground. Repeat this procedure for the other doors, then remove the tracks, brackets, and exterior trim.

Swing-up Overhead Doors

An overhead door is one that opens vertically and remains suspended overhead when open, as opposed to the swinging or sliding doors that move horizontally. A spring-loaded overhead door is one solid door that fills the entire opening. It is mounted on two large springs, one at each side of the opening, that allow the door to be easily raised while also holding it up in position when open. You will notice that the springs are fully extended when the door is down and fully retracted when the door is up.

To remove a door of this type, you need to brace it up in the open position. Open the door fully, then measure the distance between the door and the garage floor. Cut 2-×-4 braces to 1/4 inch longer than this dimension and wedge them between the floor and the door at both the front and the back. Be certain the door is securely braced before proceeding.

With the door open, the tension is off the springs, allowing them to be safely removed. Unclip the springs from the retaining brackets and remove the springs from the doors.

You will need two helpers for the next step, especially if you are working with a 16-foot door. Have your helpers stand at the front of the door (what would be the door's bottom if it were closed) and brace it in the open (up) position while you remove the 2-×-4 braces. With all three of you controlling the door, gently swing it down into the closed position.

Have your helpers stand on the outside and brace the door closed by hand, while you go inside and remove the bolts that hold the brackets to the door. With the brackets removed, you can lower the door to the ground and remove it. Finally, remove the rest of the brackets and bolts, along with the exterior trim and, if they protrude past the siding, the jambs also.

Roll-up Overhead Doors

This type of overhead door is one of the most common (FIG. 6-5). It is made up in horizontal sections, and each section is attached to a track by

Fig. 6-5. A typical sectional roll-up overhead door.

means of two rollers. A large coiled spring, mounted above the door opening and attached to the door with cables, balances the door to allow it to be easily rolled open and closed.

The difficult and dangerous part of this door removal process is unwinding the spring. You will need a stout bar or heavy screwdriver, a socket wrench, and a helper. The garage door should be closed.

Insert the bar in one of the winding holes located in the circular bracket at the end of the spring. Place tension on the bar while your helper loosens the locking bolt slightly. *Keeping solid control of the bar,* unwind the spring one-half turn, then have your helper retighten the bolt. Move the bar into the next hole, and repeat the procedure. Continue to repeat this process—slowly and carefully—until you can feel that all the tension is off the spring.

To complete the removal of the door, unbolt and remove the upper, horizontal sections of track, down past the curve. Unbolt the hinges that hold the door sections together, then with a helper, slide each individual section up until the rollers come out of the tracks (FIG. 6-6), then remove the section. Finally, remove the rest of the tracks, the spring and cables, and the exterior trim, jambs and stops (FIG. 6-7).

Fig. 6-6. Remove individual sections of the old door by unbolting them from each other and sliding them out of the tracks.

Fig. 6-7. Remove the exterior trim and door jambs.

FILLING IN THE OPENINGS

Filling in the openings left by the garage doors is actually a fairly easy framing procedure. Because headers were installed over the openings when the garage was originally built, all of the structural weight is already on those members. The framing you'll be installing does not have to be designed to be load-bearing.

In the planning sections discussed previously, you determined what you would be doing to fill the openings—door, windows, a solid wall, or a combination of these. These decisions will, of course, determine exactly how the opening will be framed in.

Framing the Opening

Begin by installing a sole plate, which will be anchored directly to the floor. This should be a 2 × 4 or 2 × 6, depending on what was used to frame the opening originally, and must be pressure-treated lumber. Cut it to length to fit in the opening and align it flush with the existing sole plates on either side of the opening. Place a thick double bead of caulk under the board, then anchor it down with lag bolts and expansion shields, or with powder-driven pins (see chapter 5).

Carefully lay out the framing on the new sole plate you installed. Mark the locations of the rough openings for the windows and doors (consult the manufacturer's specifications for the exact rough openings required), and also the locations of the studs on 16-inch center. Using a plumb bob or a long level, transfer these layout marks to the old header above the opening.

Cut your studs to length and toenail them to the sole plate and to the header. If you have window or door openings (FIGS. 6-8 to 6-10), you can use the old garage door header to span the opening without adding new headers and trimmers.

Fig. 6-8. Two single-car garage door openings have been filled in to create spaces for a door and three windows.

Fig. 6-9. Details of the framing around the window opening. The white tape around the window frame will seal and hold the new glass panes.

Fig. 6-10. Installing the new double-pane glass units. The block (bottom) temporarily holds the glass until the inside trim is installed.

Siding

You will want to match the new sheathing and siding to the original to maintain clean lines and achieve a finished appearance that doesn't look "added on." If, for example, the garage had originally been sheathed with 3/4-inch lumber, you will also want to use 3/4-inch material—whether lumber or plywood—to keep the face of the sheathings level. Install the sheathing first, cut out for the openings as necessary, then cover the sheathing with #15 felt or similar wrapping material.

Match the new siding material as close as you possibly can to the existing material (FIG. 6-11). For lap or other types of board siding, you might need to remove part of the old siding to get back to the original joints where the boards butted, or back to corners or other natural breaks. With plywood siding, remove the old sheets back to a seam from which you can start over with new sheets.

Fig. 6-11. Finish off the exterior of the old garage door openings to match the rest of the home's exterior.

Do your best to blend the new and the old together at existing seams and joints (FIG. 6-12), rather than just installing new siding and covering up the joint with some type of molding. This is what really marks a professional installation from an amateur one.

Fig. 6-12. Details of the L-flashing used at the bottom of the wall to prevent direct contact between the ground and the bottom of the last siding board.

CREATING AN OPENING INTO THE HOUSE

Unlike attic and basement remodels where access to those areas is gained via stairs from the main living area, the garage is usually at or near the same floor level as the house. While access to the converted garage could certainly be through a single doorway, perhaps even one that's already existing, most people prefer to create a larger opening that really makes the garage area feel like part of the home's overall living space.

Creating this opening means having to remove all or part of the bearing wall between the house and garage. While the basic steps are outlined here, you might wish to leave this procedure to an experienced contractor.

Bracing

The first step in the removal process is bracing the existing ceiling to take the load off the wall that's about to be removed. To do this, you'll need to construct temporary walls (FIG. 6-13) on either side of the old wall, about 3 feet back. Nail a 2-×-4 plate to the floor, parallel to the wall, and a second one to the ceiling, directly in line with the one on the floor.

Measure the distance between the plates and cut 2-×-4 studs about ⅛ inch longer. Wedge the studs firmly between the plates so that a slight upward pressure is placed against the top plate and the ceiling. Place the studs on 24- to 36-inch centers and toenail them to the plates.

Fig. 6-13. Temporary lumber supports the ceiling prior to removing the bearing wall studs.

Removing the Wall

Strip the drywall off the wall (FIG. 6-14) and off the ceiling about 18 inches back from the wall. If you encounter electrical wiring in the wall, contact your electrician to have it relocated. With a reciprocating saw and a metal-cutting blade, cut between the bottom of each stud and the bottom plate, severing the nails (FIG. 6-15). Pull the stud away from the bottom plate, then pull sharply down to pull it off the nails in the top plate. Repeat this for all the studs in the wall, then cut out and remove the top plate.

Installing the New Framing

Install a new king stud and trimmer at each end of the opening. With a helper, install a new header across the opening, resting it on the trimmers at each side of the opening. (Consult your building department for the proper size header for your situation.) The bottom of the existing joists and rafters must rest on top of the new header so that the header fully supports their weight. Reach in through the opening in the ceiling and toenail each joist and rafter onto the new header, being careful to maintain the original spacing (FIG. 6-16).

Remove the temporary walls you constructed earlier, allowing the weight of the roof and ceiling to be transferred onto the new header. Carefully remove the boards one at a time, watching for any sag in the ceiling or any other indication the new header is not taking all the weight of the old framing.

Fig. 6-14. The wall after removal of the drywall.

Fig. 6-15. *Use a reciprocating saw to sever the nails holding the studs to the plate. Note the temporary supports in the foreground.*

Fig. 6-16. *The opening following removal of the studs and installation of the header. The temporary supports are no longer needed at this point.*

FURRING AND PARTITION WALLS

Depending on the garage's intended use, you might wish to partition off the area into smaller rooms. The procedures used here are the same as those employed in the basement: pressure-treated sole plates are secured to the floor, top plates are secured to the ceiling, and wall studs are installed on 16- or 24- inch centers. Refer back to these sections in chapter 5.

There is usually very little furring that needs to be done in the garage simply because the construction and the number of exposed obstacles is different from that in a basement. One area where furring might be necessary is over exposed concrete footings—a fairly common situation in garages.

One way to cover concrete footing is to box them in by attaching pressure-treated lumber to the top and bottom of the vertical face, and at the front and back of the horizontal face. You can then apply drywall over the furring or cover it with plywood strips and then carpet up over it.

A cleaner method, although it uses up a little more interior space, is to extend studs vertically from the footing to the ceiling, creating a wall that is straight up and down with no jogs (FIG. 6-17). To do this, attach a pressure-treated 2 × 4 to the top of the footing, flush with the vertical face. Use a plumb bob to mark the ceiling, attach a second 2 × 4 to the ceiling joists, then cut and install studs between the plates. You can then drywall over the wall, extending the drywall down over the footing and attaching it with adhesive.

One other obstacle commonly encountered in the garage is the water heater. One solution is to move it to another area, but you can also build a simple and attractive enclosure for it. All you need to do is construct a partition wall along one side and a second wall with a doorway opening in it along the water heater's front. Be certain to size the enclosure and the door so the water heater can be removed should it ever need to be replaced. Finish off the walls with drywall or paneling to match the rest of the room, then install a door in the opening. The water heater is now concealed from view but easy to get to for repairs and maintenance.

Fig. 6-17. Furring out a concrete footing to create a smooth, vertical wall.

7

Insulation
and Ventilation

NEVER OVERLOOK THE NEED FOR PROPER INSULATION AND VENTILATION IN ANY remodeling project. This is especially true with attics, basements and garages. Because all three of these areas were not originally designed as living space, they will very likely be substantially underinsulated. This results in drafts, rooms that are cold in the winter and hot in the summer, and unnecessarily high heating and cooling bills. Particularly in the case of the basement, underinsulation can cause mold, mildew, and a constant clammy, damp feeling in the room.

Another important factor is noise. With these areas now being converted into living space, uninsulated walls, floors, and ceilings can make for a noisy bedroom or office.

Of equal importance with insulation is proper room ventilation. Good ventilation flushes potentially damaging moisture out of wall and ceiling cavities and removes it from living spaces. Ventilation also can flush out odors and stale air.

NORMAL INSULATION FACTORS

Recent changes in the building codes have made energy efficiency in new building and remodeling projects a greater priority, and rightfully so. A little time and effort, along with a minimal outlay of additional money, can make a building tighter, warmer, more comfortable to live in, and much less expensive to maintain.

There are several established standards for insulation that will give you some good guidelines for determining how much insulation you should have in various areas. These levels will vary with different climate zones and should be confirmed with your local building department before you begin work.

Ceilings with Attic Spaces. Ceilings with an open attic space above them, (above your garage for example), should be insulated to R-38. This is about 14 inches of blown fiberglass or 11 inches of fiberglass batts.

Vaulted and Enclosed Ceilings. If you have a vaulted ceiling with no attic above, the minimum insulation value is R-19, which is about $5^1/2$ inches of fiberglass batt. The same is true for enclosed ceilings, such as the floor between two stories of a house. If possible, increase this R-value to R-30. Using fiberglass batts, this would be about 9 inches of insulation, which will fit in a 2-×-10 joist cavity. If you have 2-×-12 joists, you might even want to go to R-38.

Walls. Current building codes required the use of R-19 insulation in exterior walls for most climate areas, which means using a 2-×-6 stud wall. R-11 was the long-time standard; if you have existing 2-×-4 walls in your garage or basement, the inspectors will probably allow you to stick with R-11 because R-19 won't fit in those cavities.

If you are furring out concrete walls in the basement, you might want to use rigid foam insulation. Although it's more expensive, it has a higher R-value per inch, so you can get more insulation in a smaller cavity. Some of the better foam insulation boards have R-values in excess of R-7 per inch.

Floors. R-19 is the standard for floors also. Once again, if you have the joist cavity space, use a higher R-value insulation.

INSULATION MATERIALS

Insulation comes in a variety of forms and materials, each with different R-values and applications. Most are readily available from your building materials dealer, who can assist you in selecting the best one for your particular application.

Fiberglass is probably the most common of the insulation materials, both for professional and do-it-yourself installations. Fiberglass is available in batts and blankets (FIG. 7-1), which are long strips of insulation either in a roll or in precut pieces, usually with a vapor barrier attached. It is also available in loose fill that is blown by machine into attic spaces. Fiberglass has an R-value of approximately 3.1 per inch in batts, and 2.2 per inch in loose fill.

Cellulose, another common insulating material, is available as a loose fill material only, for blowing into attics. Unlike fiberglass, cellulose blowing machines can be rented, and installation is easy for the do-it-yourselfer. Cellulose has an R-value of approximately 3.7 per inch.

Fig. 7-1. Fiberglass blanket insulation between furring boards. Note the vapor barrier on the face of the sheets, which must face into the room.

Rigid insulation boards are made up from a variety of materials (FIG. 7-2), that are formed into dense sheets of uniform thickness. Common rigid board materials include *expanded polystyrene*, which is a brittle, white, beaded material, also commonly used in making coolers and similar items; *extruded polystyrene*, which is much denser and stronger, has a higher R-value, and is approved for use below ground; and *polyisocyanurate*, another dense board with a very high R-value. Common sheet sizes for these materials are 2 feet × 8 feet and 4 feet × 8 feet, with thicknesses of $1/2$, $3/4$, 1, $1^1/2$, and 2 inches commonly available. R-values vary between materials and manufacturers and can be as high as R-7 per inch.

(COURTESY OF CELOTEX CORPORATION)

Fig. 7-2. A variety of rigid insulation boards.

VAPOR BARRIERS

The air inside your house contains moisture in the form of water vapor, which is picked up from cooking, washing, breathing, and other sources. Warm air is always trying to move toward colder surfaces and is, therefore, attracted to exterior walls. As the warm, moisture-laden air tries to pass through to the outside, its moisture will condense against cold surfaces and turn to water. A commonly visible example of this is condensation on cold windows in the winter, which then turns to frost if the window is cold enough.

If condensation happens in your walls and attic, deposits of moisture could do serious damage to wooden framing members. To prevent this, you must provide a vapor barrier to keep the moisture from reaching the interior cavity.

Vapor barriers are usually incorporated into batt insulation in the form of a foil or kraft paper facing over the insulation. When using this type of insulation, always be certain that the vapor barrier is facing the *heated* side of the wall, floor, or ceiling. For example: in a wall, the vapor barrier faces into the room, not toward the outside of the house; in a floor, the vapor barrier faces up toward the heated room; in an attic, the vapor barrier faces down toward the heated rooms.

Plastic sheeting (FIGS. 7-3 and 7-4) is also commonly used as a vapor barrier over *unfaced* insulation. (It cannot be used over faced insulation because it would create a double vapor barrier, and moisture could become trapped between the two.) Plastic sheeting works especially well in vaulted ceilings, where a good, continuous vapor barrier is especially important. Be sure and use clear plastic, not black, so that you don't obscure the studs or joists and make them difficult to locate when installing the drywall.

AREAS TO INSULATE

When deciding which areas to insulate, always keep in mind that you are striving to prevent warm air from moving to cold surfaces. This visualization will help you spot areas you might otherwise overlook, such as heating ducts. Remember also that virtually every type of insulation is flammable to some degree and must be covered with a minimum of 1/2-inch gypsum wallboard or other material on the living space side.

The following specific list of areas and suggested R-values should help also:

Attic—R-30 to R-45. Attic spaces over heated rooms can be insulated with blown or batt insulation (FIG. 7-5).

Vaulted Ceiling—R-19 to R-38. Vaulted ceilings are usually insulated with batt insulation placed between the rafters. Most codes require a vaulted ceiling to be ventilated by maintaining a 1-inch air space over the top of the

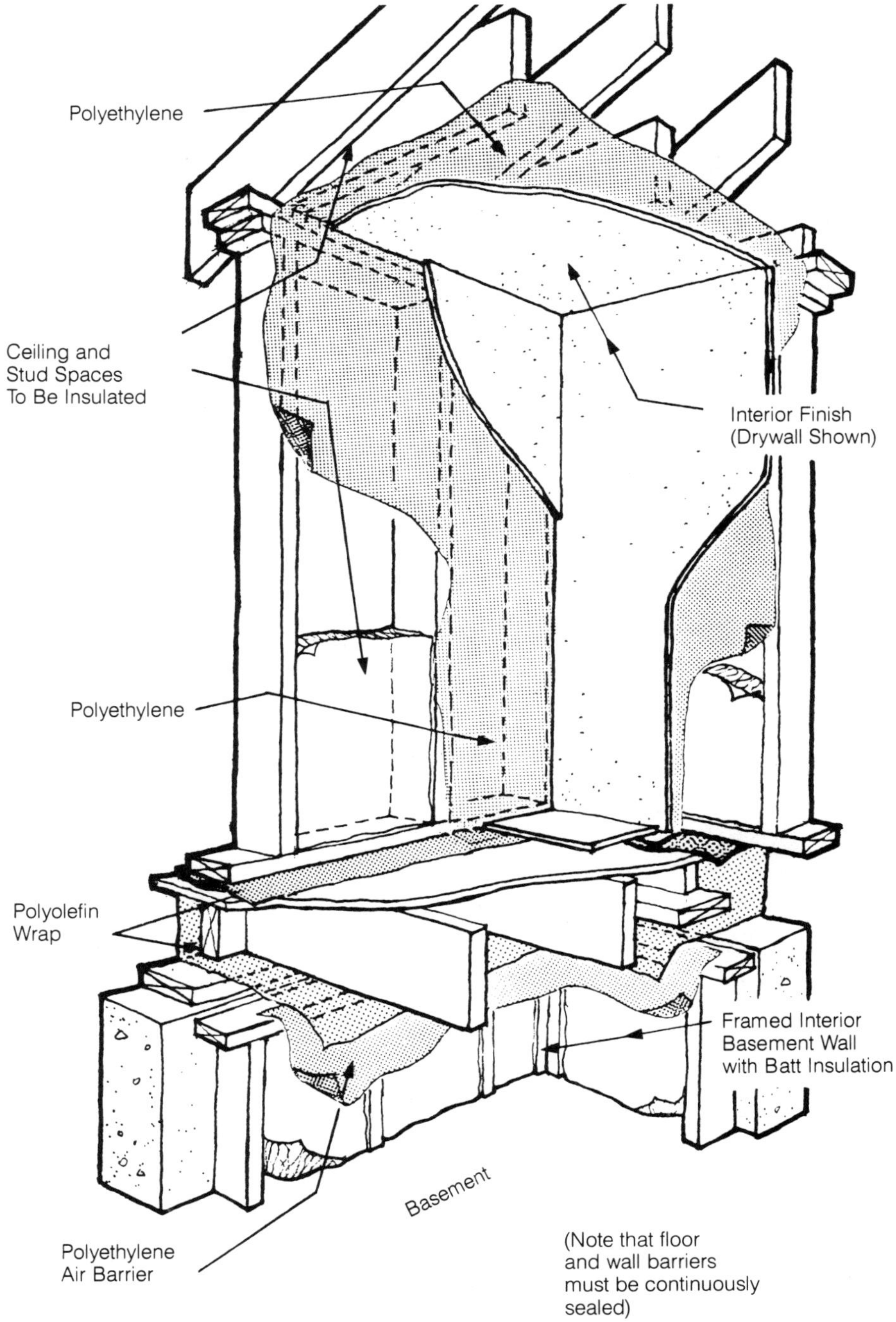

Polyethylene

Ceiling and
Stud Spaces
To Be Insulated

Interior Finish
(Drywall Shown)

Polyethylene

Polyolefin
Wrap

Framed Interior
Basement Wall
with Batt Insulation

Basement

Polyethylene
Air Barrier

(Note that floor
and wall barriers
must be continuously
sealed)

Fig. 7-3. A vapor barrier constructed from plastic sheeting.

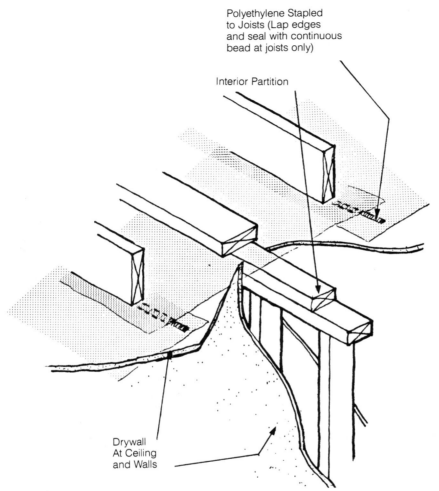

Polyethylene Stapled
to Joists (Lap edges
and seal with continuous
bead at joists only)

Interior Partition

Drywall
At Ceiling
and Walls

Fig. 7-4. Details of how the sheeting is overlapped over the top of a partition wall.

insulation. This air space will limit the amount of insulation you can place in the cavity, depending on the height of the rafters (FIGS. 7-6 and 7-7).

Roof—R-19 to R-22. If you have an exposed ceiling of wood or other material that does not have a cavity to insulate, an alternative is to insulate the roof. Use a rigid insulation board placed between furring strips on 24-inch centers, then install new sheathing and roofing (FIG. 7-8).

Cavity Walls—R-11 to R-22. Open wall cavities, such as newly framed walls, are easily insulated with fiberglass batts. Fill the cavity completely (a 2-×-6 wall can accommodate two R-11 batts for a little additional insulation value) and keep the vapor barrier to the heated side of the wall.

Fig. 7-5. Use a piece of fiber-glass batt insulation on a knee wall door.

Fig. 7-6. Use foil-faced fiberglass batt insulation in a vaulted ceiling.

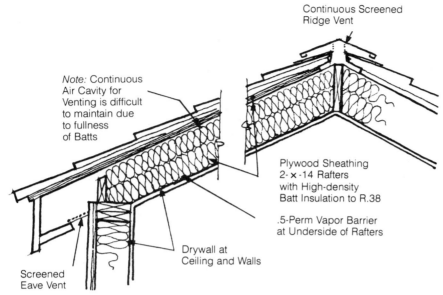

Continuous Screened
Ridge Vent

Note: Continuous
Air Cavity for
Venting is difficult
to maintain due
to fullness
of Batts

Plywood Sheathing
2- x -14 Rafters
with High-density
Batt Insulation to R.38

.5-Perm Vapor Barrier
at Underside of Rafters

Drywall at
Ceiling and Walls

Screened
Eave Vent

Fig. 7-7. Cavity insulation in a vaulted ceiling.

Fig. 7-8. A typical roof insulation installation. Rigid boards are installed between 2- × -4 furring strips. then covered with new sheathing.

Solid Walls—R-9 to R-15. Insulate solid wall surfaces without cavities, such as concrete or concrete block walls, with rigid boards. If the wall is smooth and solid, glue the insulation boards directly to the wall (FIG. 7-9), then glue the wallboard to the insulation. Be sure and use an adhesive that is approved for the type of insulation you're installing. The alternative method is to install furring strips, usually 2 × 4s installed flat on 24-inch centers, then place rigid insulation between the furring and cover with wallboard (FIGS. 7-10 and 7-11).

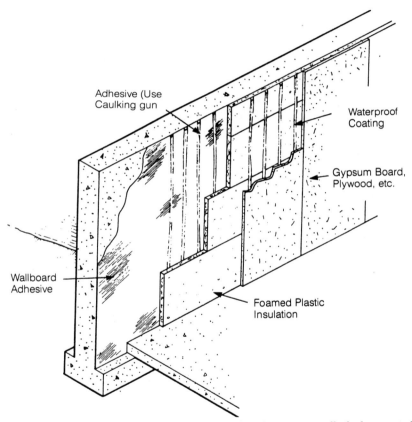

Fig. 7-9. *Rigid insulation sheets that have been glued to the concrete wall of a basement. Be certain to use adhesive that is compatible with the type of insulation being used.*

Floors—R-19 to R-38. Batt insulation can easily be placed between floor joists to the full depth of the cavity. Keep the vapor barrier up toward the heated space. Floors between heated spaces, such as between an attic and the living space below, do not need to be insulated for heat loss. Insulation placed between the joists, however, will greatly reduce sound transmission between floors.

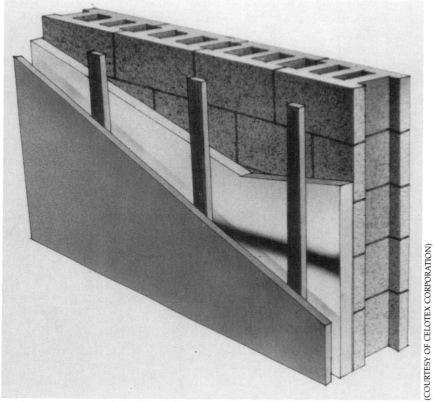

(COURTESY OF CELOTEX CORPORATION)

Fig. 7-10. Another method of insulating concrete block walls is to apply wood furring strips over the rigid insulation instead of directly on the block wall.

Knee Walls—R-11 to R-22. The space between the studs in an attic knee wall is treated just like any other wall cavity (see "Walls" above). Remember to also insulate the horizontal floor area behind the knee wall, using batts or blown insulation.

Ducts and Pipes—R-11. Insulate heating ducts and water or hydronic pipes (pipes used in hot-water or steam heating systems) to reduce heat loss to the surrounding area. Wrap ducts with fiberglass batts and insulate pipes with fiberglass or prefabricated foam pipe wraps.

Skylight Shafts—R-11 to R-22. Don't overlook the importance of insulating the shaft between a skylight and the living space below. Use batt insulation on the attic side of the shaft, with the vapor barrier facing the inside of the shaft. You can also box the shaft with rigid board on the attic side.

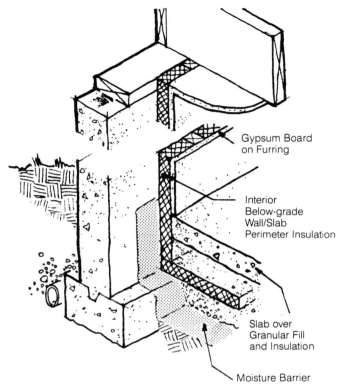

Gypsum Board
on Furring

Interior
Below-grade
Wall/Slab
Perimeter Insulation

Slab over
Granular Fill
and Insulation

Moisture Barrier

Fig. 7-11. The proper method of installing insulation and a vapor barrier in a newly constructed basement.

ATTIC VENTILATION

To ventilate an attic, you must create a flow of air that brings fresh outside air into the space and exhausts hot stale air out. You can create this flow in two ways: through natural convection or through the use of power fans.

Natural Convection Ventilation

You can achieve natural convection ventilation by using intake and exhaust vents (FIG. 7-12). *Low vents*, placed in the soffits or between the rafters where they sit on the wall plates, allow cool air to enter the attic. *High vents*, in the form of roof jacks, gable end vents (FIG. 7-13), or continuous ridge vents (FIG. 7-14), allow warm air to escape. The escaping air creates a vacuum behind it, which acts to draw more cool air in through the low vents, creating a continuous cycle of ventilation (FIG. 7-15).

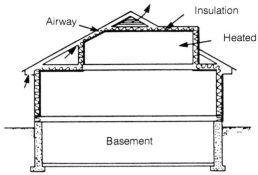

Fig. 7-12. An example of how an "envelope" of insulation is formed around the heated portion of a house. The insulation is continuous up the first-story walls, across the ceiling, up the knee walls, and across the dormer and attic ceiling.

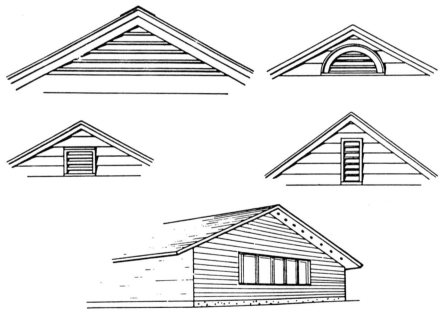

Fig. 7-13. Common gable vent configurations.

When using both high and low vents, the building codes call for a ventilation ratio of 1 square foot of vent area for each 300 square feet of attic area, equally divided between the high and low vents. These ventilation requirements apply to the unheated portion of the attic, not attic areas that have been converted for living space. Included in this would be the attic over a garage and those attic areas not being converted to heated living space, such as the storage areas behind the knee walls.

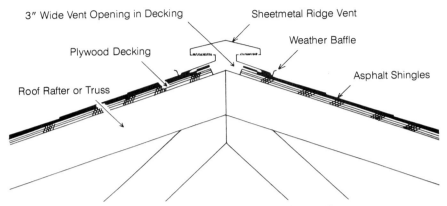

Fig. 7-14. A premanufactured, continuous ridge ventilator.

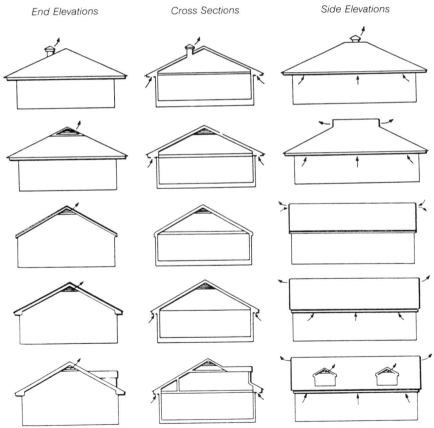

Fig. 7-15. Examples of the natural convective flow of ventilation through high and low vents in various roof and ceiling configurations.

For example, if your attic is 1,200 square feet in area, you would need 4 square feet of vent area (1,200/300). Divide this equally between high and low vents, and you would need 2 square feet of high vent and 2 square feet of low vent. To convert this to square inches, the way most vents are sold, divide by 144.

Power Fan Ventilation

Power fans ventilate by using wind or electrically powered fans (FIGS. 7-16 and 7-17) to create a flow of ventilating air in the attic. These fans, placed high on the roof, pull hot air out of the attic and create a vacuum behind them. This vacuum draws in cooler air from the outside, creating a ventilation flow.

With any type of power fan, you still need low vents to allow the outside air a way into the attic. A good ratio for low vents when using power fans would be 1 square foot of vent for every 150 to 200 square feet of attic space.

Power Roof Fans. This is an electrically powered fan that is mounted on the roof up near the ridge. Installation requires removing some shingles in the area where the unit is to sit; cutting a hole through the sheathing; mounting the unit and patching the shingles; then connecting the fan to 120-volt power (no separate circuit is required for most units). Roof fans can be controlled by a simple switch arrangement, by an attic thermostat that activates the unit at a preset temperature, or by a humidistat that activates the unit at a preset humidity level in the attic.

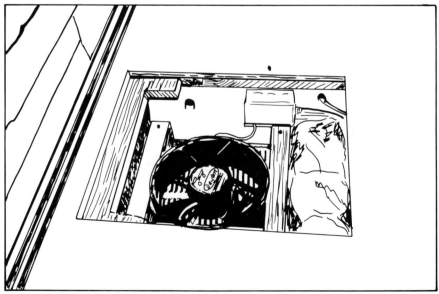

Fig. 7-16. A power ventilating fan placed in the floor between a heated basement and the living space above. The fan helps circulate warm air from the basement into the upper portion of the house.

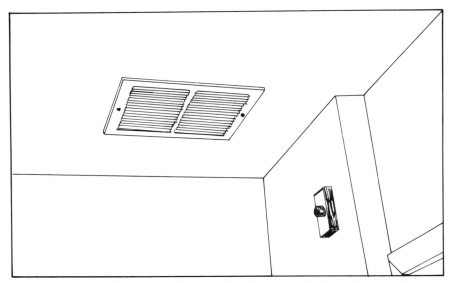

Fig. 7-17. The same fan in Fig. 7-16 as seen from the basement side. Note the speed control mounted on the wall at the lower right.

Power Gable Fans. Power gable fans are essentially the same as roof fans except that they mount high in the gable end wall, as close to the ridge as possible. They are a little easier to install in most situations, as no cutting of the roof is necessary.

Wind Turbines. Wind turbines mount on the roof at the ridge and are installed just like the power roof fans. They utilize a slotted, revolving cap over a short, round, sheet-metal duct. Wind blowing across the cap catches the slots and turns the unit, creating an air flow. These units have lost some of their popularity in recent years because they are rather obtrusive on the roof and, as tests have shown, are only slightly more effective than regular passive high vents.

Vaulted Ceilings

As mentioned under "Vaulted Ceilings" in the previous insulation section, you must ventilate enclosed areas with no accessible attic space, such as a vaulted ceiling, to prevent the buildup of dangerous moisture. To do this, you must maintain a 1- to $1^1/2$-inch airspace over the top of the insulation (FIG. 7-18) and provide vents at the bottom and top of the cavity (FIG. 7-19). If there is solid, midspan blocking between the rafters, drill out the blocking to permit the passage of air.

Venting presents some obvious problems when dealing with a large enclosed area. You must place the insulation carefully so it doesn't bulge up and close off the air passage. Also, you must place the vents so that *each and*

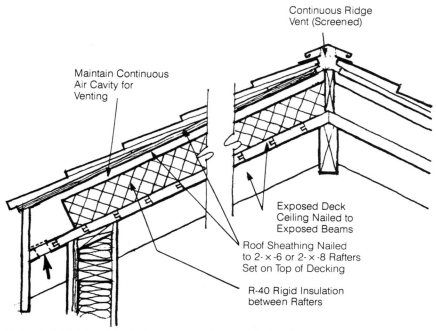

Continuous Ridge
Vent (Screened)

Maintain Continuous
Air Cavity for
Venting

Exposed Deck
Ceiling Nailed to
Exposed Beams

Roof Sheathing Nailed
to 2- × -6 or 2- × -8 Rafters
Set on Top of Decking

R-40 Rigid Insulation
between Rafters

Fig. 7-18. *Maintain a 1-inch air cavity over the top of the insulation in a vaulted ceiling. Note the continuous soffit vent (arrow at lower left) and the continuous ridge vent, which greatly simplify providing the ventilating air.*

every cavity has ventilation. The easiest way of achieving this is to use continuous ridge and soffit ventilation, which looks nice, is relatively easy to install, and provides air openings between all the rafter spaces. Consult with your building materials supplier for the proper type of vent arrangement for your situation.

Because of the problems associated with maintaining a continuous airspace in enclosed areas, some local codes have been revised to allow the entire cavity between the rafters to be filled with insulation as long as a continuous vapor barrier is used. This is normally achieved by packing the cavity with unfaced insulation, then covering the entire ceiling with clear plastic sheeting before installing the finished ceiling. This is a much easier installation and allows greater insulation depth, so check with your local building officials to see if this is permissible in your area.

SPOT VENTILATION

In areas such as the basement, where attic-type convection ventilation is not practical, you can provide spot ventilation with electrically operated fans (FIG. 7-20). Use fans in high-moisture locations, such as bathroom and laun-

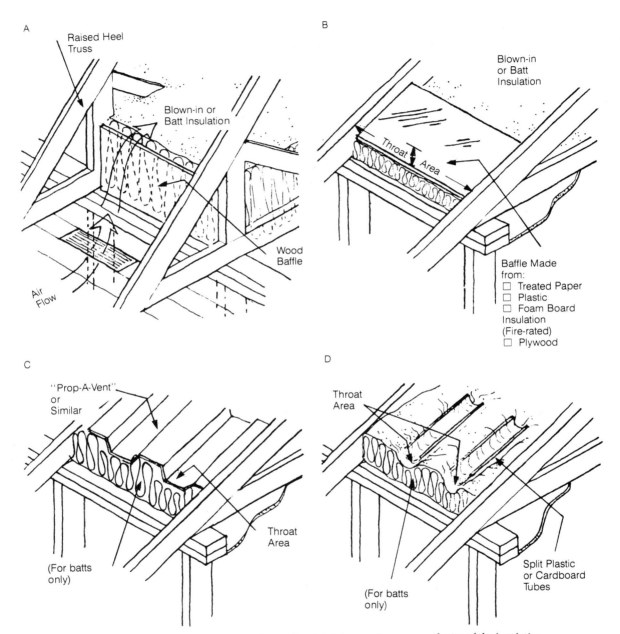

Fig. 7-19. Common methods of providing and maintaining an airspace over the top of the insulation.

Fig. 7-20. *A power ventilating fan (square opening) installed in a vaulted ceiling. The round opening is for a recessed light.*

dry areas and duct them to the outside to carry the moisture completely clear of the house.

When sizing a ventilation fan, plan on providing 10-to-12 air changes per hour (ACH). The following example is based on a 10-foot-×-10-foot room with an 8-foot high ceiling:

$$10 \times 10 \times 8 = 800 \text{ cubic feet of air in the room}$$
$$800 \text{ CF} \times 12 \text{ ACH} = 9600 \text{ cubic feet per hour (CFH)}$$

Because most fans are rated in cubic feet per minute (CFM), divide by 60 to make the conversion:

$$9600 \text{ CFH}/60 = 160 \text{ CFM}$$

The other consideration when selecting a ventilating fan is the noise level. Fans are rated in *sones,* with one sone being roughly equal to the sound level of a quiet refrigerator running in a quiet kitchen. The lower the sone rating, the quieter the fan will be. Most ventilation fans in the CFM range you would be looking for average 2 to 5 sones.

8

Stair Construction

ONE THING THAT ALL ATTIC AND BASEMENT REMODELING PROJECTS HAVE IN
common is the need for stairs. In many instances, particularly with a basement, those stairs are already in place (FIGS. 8-1 and 8-2) but are undersized or
uncomfortably designed to serve the increased traffic that comes with the
new living space. Many attics might not have any stairway at all, so you'll
need to consider how and where to construct a new one.

Stair construction is governed by a variety of building codes, conventional construction practices, and "rules of thumb" that might seem a little
confusing at first. While an intricate set of stairs might be out of the range of
your expertise, most straight stairs and their related trim can be handled by
any experienced home carpenter.

TYPES OF STAIRS

Stairs are classified by their layout and the direction of their travel from one
floor to the next (FIG. 8-3). Some common examples are:

Straight stairs, as the name implies, run in a straight line between two
floors. This is the simplest set of stairs to construct but requires the most
straight-line distance.

Platform stairs use one or more platforms, called *landings*, to break up the
run and change the direction of travel. If one landing is used, resulting in a
90-degree change of direction, the stair layout is referred to as an L; two landings with a 180-degree change of direction result in a U-shape stair. Platform

Fig. 8-1. An existing set of basement stairs with landing.

Fig. 8-2. The same stairs as Fig. 8-1 are now dressed up with carpeting and a fresh coat of paint.

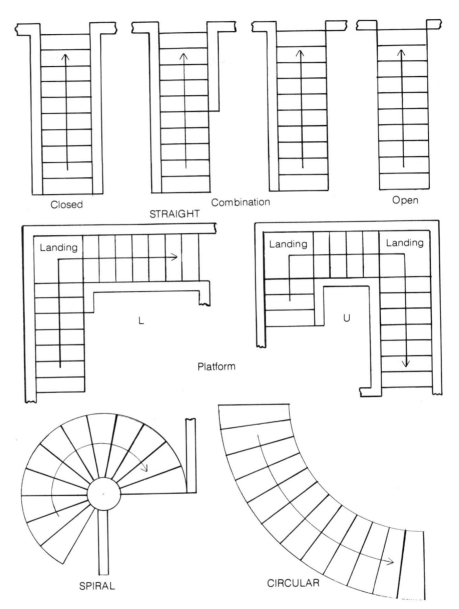

Fig. 8-3. Common stair configurations.

stairs are similar to straight stairs in construction, but the landing allows the stairs to fit into an area where a long run is not available.

Circular stairs curve gently from one floor to the next. They might encompass direction changes of less than 90 degrees up to a full 360 degrees, but rarely beyond one full revolution. These are more difficult to construct than straight or platform stairs, require a large amount of space, and are usually reserved for main entrance stairways only.

Winding stairs (FIG. 8-4) are somewhat similar to an L-shaped platform stair in that they are constructed along two adjacent walls and turn a corner at 90 degrees. Instead of a single large landing, wedge-shaped treads are used to turn the corner in a semicircular manner, allowing more rise per foot of run than the platform stairs do. Winders are fairly difficult to build but allow a stairway to be placed in a confined area.

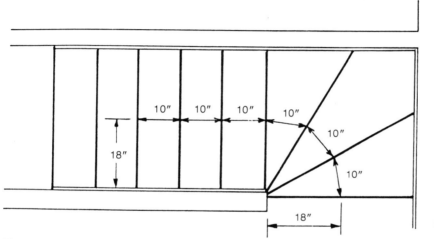

Fig. 8-4. Winder stairs, showing the minimum recommended tread width.

Spiral stairs differ somewhat from circular stairs. Spiral stairs revolve tightly around a center pole and might involve several complete revolutions between floors. This is the most difficult of all the stair types to construct, but entire units can be purchased prefabricated to your specifications. Spiral stairs take up the least amount of floor space but are subject to a variety of building code restrictions.

Open stairs have no wall on one or both sides of the stairway. *Closed stairs* have a solid wall on one or both sides. *Combination stairs* have a combination of both open and closed.

Service stairs serve nonliving space portions of the house, such as unoccupied basements or attics.

BUILDING CODES AND STANDARD PRACTICES

Before beginning the design and construction sequences of your new stairs, it helps to know stair layout terms, what building codes are required, and how professional carpenters on the job would normally undertake stair layout and construction.

Stair Terminology

FIGURES 8-5 to 8-7 illustrate the parts of a stairway as well as the terms and clearances of the layout and construction.

Rise—the total vertical distance a stairway travels from one floor to the next floor.

Run—the total horizontal distance that the stairway travels.

Unit Rise—the vertical height of one individual step.

Unit Run—the horizontal depth of one individual step.

Tread—a single horizontal step, or the board that makes up that step.

Riser—a single vertical board spanning the distance between the top of one step and the bottom of the next.

Nosing—the portion of the tread, usually rounded, that overhangs the riser below it.

Head room—the total vertical clearance between a step and the ceiling above it, measured at its lowest point.

Stringer—the notched board that the individual stairs are attached to.

Carriage—the complete system of stringers and other supports that carry the weight of the entire stair assembly.

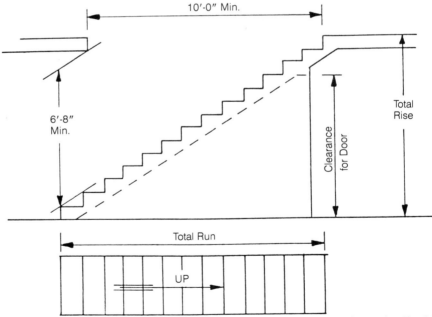

Fig. 8-5. Terms and clearances associated with the layout and construction of a set of residential stairs.

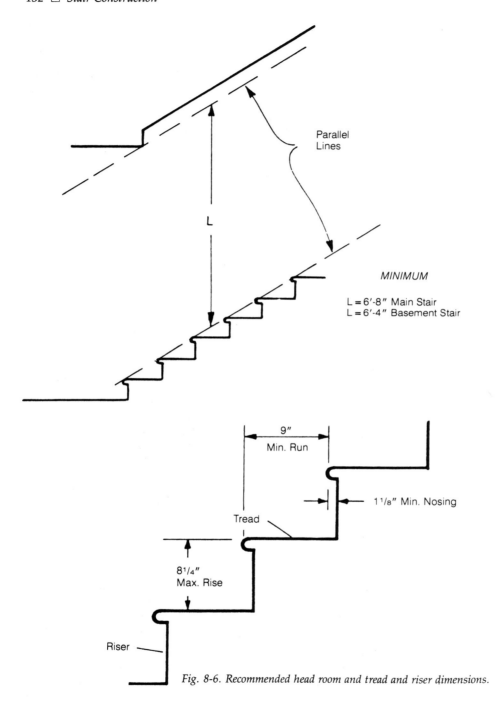

Parallel
Lines

MINIMUM

L = 6'-8" Main Stair
L = 6'-4" Basement Stair

9"
Min. Run

1 1/8" Min. Nosing

Tread

8 1/4"
Max. Rise

Riser

Fig. 8-6. Recommended head room and tread and riser dimensions.

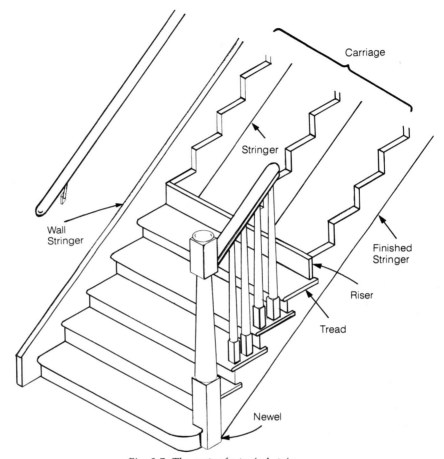

Fig. 8-7. The parts of a typical stairway.

Building Code Requirements

To ensure safety and comfort, the building codes have established certain uniform criteria for the construction of stairs. If you have an existing set of stairs serving an attic or basement that falls below the minimum standards, but existing conditions will not allow you to upgrade them, the building officials will probably allow you to go on using those stairs. Consult with them to determine what their requirements and restrictions will be.

Unit Rise. Each step shall not be less than 4 inches nor greater than 8 inches (approximately 7 to 7½ inches is preferred).

Unit Run. The minimum horizontal run of each stair is 9 inches (approximately 10 to 11 inches is preferred).

Winding Stairs. The minimum 9-inch-wide run must be present at a point not more than 12 inches from the wall of the stairway, measured from the wall where the stairs are narrowest. At no point can the stairs have a unit run of less than 6 inches.

Spiral Stairs. The tread must provide a clear walking area of 26 inches from column to handrail. The unit run must be at least $7^{1}/_{2}$ inches wide at a point 12 inches in from the column. The unit rise cannot exceed $9^{1}/_{2}$ inches and must allow for a minimum head room of $6^{1}/_{2}$ feet. Normal diameters are 4, 5, and 6 feet. Spiral stairs are limited by most codes to areas that serve 400 square feet or less; check with the local building department for specific limitations in your area.

Landings. The measurement of a landing in the direction of travel must be at least as much as the width of the stairway, except for landings on straight stairs, where the dimension of the landing in the direction of the run need not exceed 4 feet. A door swinging over the landing cannot reduce the landing's width by more than one half.

Stairway Width. For most applications, the stairway must be at least 30 inches wide (try and keep to a minimum of at least 36 inches wherever possible). Handrails are also required on at least one side of the stairs. As long as they do not protrude more than 6 inches from the wall, they are not counted against the stairway's minimum width.

Head Room. Minimum head room is $6^{1}/_{2}$ feet, with $6^{2}/_{3}$ feet preferred.

Standard Practices

It is the ratio of the stair's rise to its run that makes a stairway feel comfortable underfoot. For example, using a rise of 4 inches and run of 12 inches will make the stairs long and shallow, using up a lot of floor space and making the step up feel very awkward. Using a 9-inch rise and a 9-inch run will minimize the horizontal travel of the stairway but will make it feel very steep and dangerous.

Over the years, carpenters have developed standard practices that set the relationship between unit rise and unit run within certain limits that ensure comfort and safety. These are not building codes but rather "rules of thumb" to help with your stair layout and design:

Rule 1: If you add the height of two risers plus one tread, the result should be approximately 25 inches (Example: 7-inch riser and 11-inch tread: 7 + 7 + 11 = 25)

Rule 2: Adding one riser and one tread should equal approximately 17 to 18 inches (From the above example: 7 + 11 = 18).

DESIGNING A STAIRWAY

If your attic or basement already has an interior stairway, it might be usable as is. If one does not already exist, however, you're faced with the problem of designing one and figuring out where to put it.

As mentioned previously, different stairway configurations have different space requirements. A set of straight stairs requires the most length but the least width; platform stairs require less length but must be placed along two or more adjacent walls, and so require more width; a spiral staircase takes the least amount of floor space but is expensive and will not serve large areas.

Selecting a Location

There are several factors that go into selecting the stairway's location. First, it must be in an area of the main floor that is not in the way and does not interfere with normal traffic patterns. It needs to enter the basement or attic in a similarly convenient location. In the case of the attic, it must enter the room in an area that is not directly underneath the slope of the roof to ensure adequate head room.

Second, you also need to have enough room in both areas to handle the run of the stairway. The more room you have, the easier it is to lay out the stairway and keep it from being too steep or having too many jogs and turns.

Finally, the stairs must begin and end in accessible areas. Having the stairs start in the master bedroom or end up outside the door to the bathroom is obviously not desirable.

The best way to begin, and the method most designers and contractors use when selecting a stairway location, is to make a scale drawing of both the main floor and the attic or basement. Use the same scale for both drawings and draw them in pencil on tracing paper. Now, lay one drawing over the top of the other one and align them to each other. This will enable you to try out various locations on the main floor and see where they fall in the attic or basement.

Try out several different locations. Initially, concerning yourself with where the stairs are on the main floor. If a straight run will not work, try a 90-degree or 180-degree set of platform stairs, or even spiral stairs of various diameters.

Calculating Rise and Run

To figure the overall rise and run, a couple of simple measurements are needed. First, measure from one finished floor to the next finished floor, including the thickness of the floor joists and the finish flooring material. This dimension is the *overall rise*, or vertical height, of the stairway.

Next, determine the number of individual steps you want to use—10 to 15 steps is normal for most stairways—then perform some calculations to see how the stairs lay out. For example, let's assume you would like to use 13 steps in the stairway and that you have 9 feet between the floor of the living room, where the stairs will begin, and the floor of the attic where they will end:

$$9 \text{ feet} \times 12 = 108 \text{ inches}$$
$$108 \text{ inches}/13 \text{ steps} = 8.3 \text{ inches of rise per step}$$

Because this makes each step too high, try again with 14 or 15 steps:

$$108/14 = 7.7 \text{ inches}$$
$$108/15 = 7.2 \text{ inches}$$

Using a unit rise of 7.2 or approximately $7^1/4$ inches, would make the most comfortable stairs, so you would plan on using 15 steps. If space is limited, you could use 14 steps at $7^3/4$ inches each.

Next, determine the width of each tread, using one of the rules of thumb discussed previously. For a $7^1/4$ inch riser, Rule 1 gives you a tread width of 10.5 inches (2 risers + 1 tread = 25, so 25 − 7.25 − 7.25 = 10.5 inches). Rule 2, where one riser plus one tread should fall between 17 and 18, checks out also (7.25 + 10.5 = 17.75).

Now, you can determine the total run of the stairway by multiplying the number of steps by the width of each tread:

$$15 \text{ steps} \times 10.5 \text{ inches} = 157.5 \text{ inches} =$$
$$13 \text{ feet } 1^1/2 \text{ inches of total run.}$$

FRAMING THE FLOOR OPENING

For a new set of stairs, you need to frame an opening in the floor to accommodate them (FIG. 8-8). The size of the hole is dictated by the width and length of the stairway.

Make a scale drawing of the stairway as viewed from the side. Measuring down from the ceiling to the stairs, you can determine how long the opening in the floor needs to be to provide the necessary head room.

To construct the opening (FIG. 8-9), cut the joists and box them in with doubled headers. First, install single headers across the cut ends of the joists, leaving an opening that is 3 inches longer than needed. Next, install single trimmers that run parallel with the joists, creating an opening that is 3 inches wider than needed. Finally, double the headers and trimmers to leave a rough opening that is the proper size.

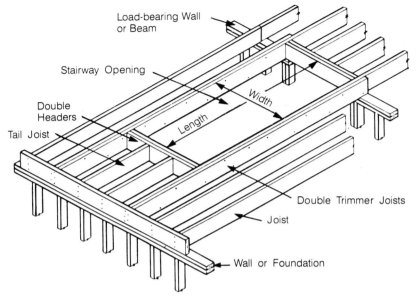

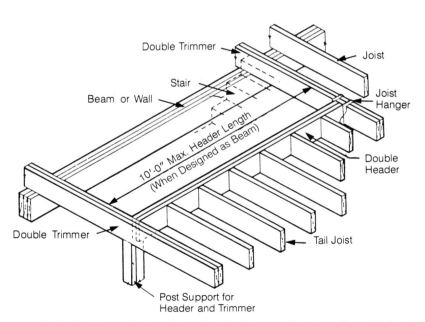

Fig. 8-8. The framing layout for the stair opening in a floor or ceiling depends on whether the joists are running parallel with the opening (top) or perpendicular (bottom).

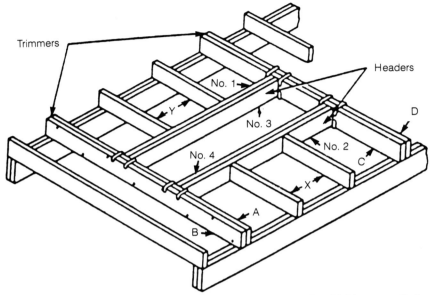

Fig. 8-9. The framing sequence for constructing the opening. The joists (X, Y) are cut off, then the doubled trimmers are installed (A – D), followed by the doubled headers (1 – 4).

BASIC STAIR CONSTRUCTION

Laying out the stringers is the hardest part of the entire stair construction process, and even that just takes a little patience. Begin by selecting a straight, defect-free piece of 2 × 12 for the first stringer. Set it up on a pair of sawhorses.

Measure the exact rise between floors and mark this dimension out on one edge of the stringer. Next, set a pair of dividers to the unit rise determined earlier (7.25 inches in the example) and lay off 15 stairs of that height along the edge of the stringer. If the last layout falls short of the total rise mark you made earlier, open the dividers slightly and try the layout again. If the last layout is too long, shorten the dividers. Keep experimenting until your last layout with the dividers falls exactly on the total rise mark. Measure the distance between the points of the dividers, and this will be the exact riser height you'll be using.

Measure and mark the riser height (FIG. 8-10) on the tongue (the short arm) of a framing square, then measure and mark the tread width on the body of the square (the long arm). Clamp a straight piece of wood between the two points. Set the board against the edge of the stringer, at what will be the top, and draw a pencil line along the edge of the framing square. Move the square down to where the pencil line met the edge of the stringer, and make another pencil line. Repeat this until all the steps have been laid off.

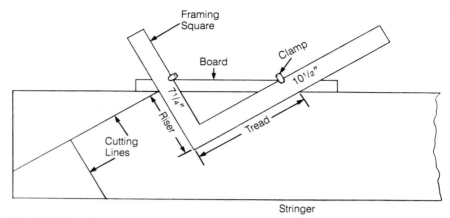

Fig. 8-10. *Use a framing square to lay out the tread and riser cuts for a stair stringer. The block of wood clamped to the square maintains accuracy for the repetitive layouts of the notches.*

Because the stringer begins with a riser, extend the last line back to indicate where the stringer needs to be cut off at the floor (FIG. 8-11). The tread and riser lines at the top of the stringer should also be extended to the back edge of the board. Finally, you need to mark off the thickness of one tread at the bottom of the stringer layout. This will allow for the thickness of the tread lumber and will make the layout come out correctly at the top.

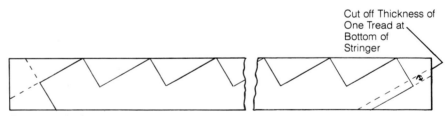

Fig. 8-11. *The fully laid out stringer, prior to cutting. Notice how the cutting lines have been extended top and bottom to the edges of the board, and how the bottom of the stringer has been marked to remove the thickness of one tread.*

Use a handsaw or circular saw to cut along the pencil lines, creating notches in the stringer. If you are using a circular saw, finish the cuts with a handsaw so you do not overcut the notches and weaken the stringer. Three stringers typically make up a complete carrige for residential stairs. Test fit this first stringer you cut, then use it as a pattern to cut the rest.

Depending on your method of attachment (FIGS. 8-12 and 8-13), cut notches at the top and bottom of the back edge of the carriage to receive the blocking that will hold it in place. Prefabricated joist hangers also can be used at the top of the carriage to secure it to the floor header. Toenail the bottom blocking to the subfloor.

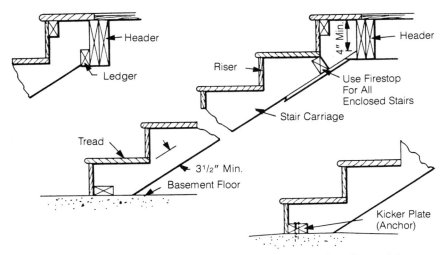

Header

Ledger

Riser

4" Min.

Header

Use Firestop
For All
Enclosed Stairs

Stair Carriage

Tread

3¹/₂" Min.

Basement Floor

Kicker Plate
(Anchor)

Fig. 8-12. Standard methods of attaching the stair carriage to the ceiling and floor.

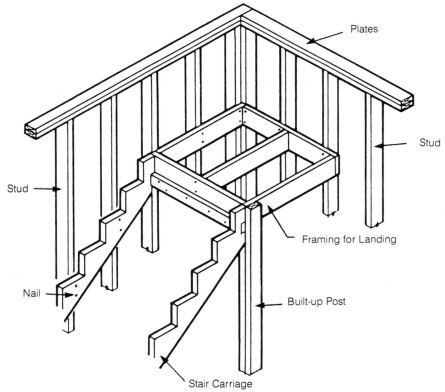

Plates

Stud

Stud

Framing for Landing

Nail

Built-up Post

Stair Carriage

Fig. 8-13. Framing a carriage and landing arrangement for a set of platform stairs.

FINISHING THE STAIRWAY

How you choose to finish the stairway is a matter of personal preference. If you intend to carpet the stairs, you can make the treads out of ³/₄-inch plywood. If the treads are to be exposed, select ³/₄- or 1-inch oak, maple, or other hardwood lumber, and round over the edge of the nosing.

Most closed stairways use a piece of lumber between the edge of the treads and the wall, called a *finished stringer*, or *wall stringer* (FIG. 8-14). There are a couple of ways of installing this piece, but probably the easiest is to leave a ³/₄-inch gap between the stringer and the face of the finished wall (FIG. 8-15). When rough framing is complete, slip the wall string into place and secure it to the rough stringer or the wall, then install the treads. For an open stairway, cut a finished string to match the shape of the outside rough stringer, then mount it to the stringer's face to give a finished appearance.

For closed stairs, finish off the installation by mounting a handrail to the wall on handrail brackets, which can be purchased prefabricated or build from wood. On open stairs, use a baluster and handrail arangement that terminates in a strong post at the beginning and end of the staircase. The posts are known as *newel posts,* and the entire assembly of balusters, handrail, and newels is the *balustrade* (FIG. 8-16).

There are several manufacturers of prefabricated balustrade parts in a variety of styles and types of wood, and most are designed for simple, strong installation by the do-it-yourselfer. Check with your building materials dealer for a look at what's available.

The stairs also offer a number of storage opportunities. Shelves and bins can be tucked in under the stringers (FIG. 8-17) or at the wall where a landing turns (FIG. 8-18).

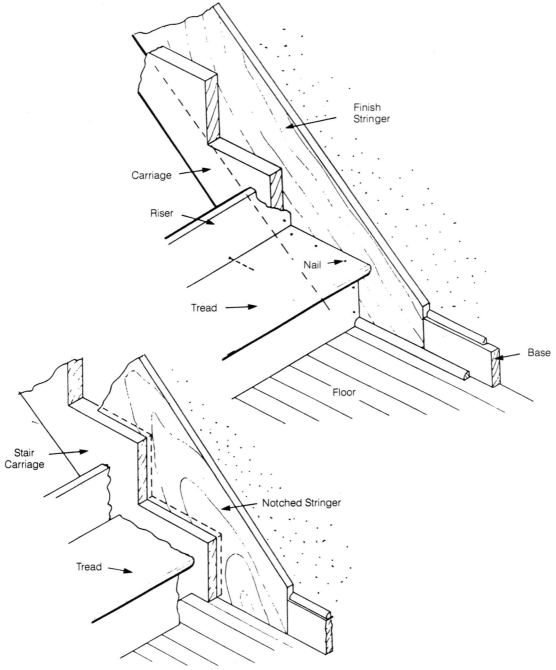

Fig. 8-14. *Two methods of installing the finished wall stringer on a closed set of stairs.*

Fig. 8-15. Use a rough 1 × 4 to maintain clearance between the side of a stair carriage and the wall, which allows you to insert the wall stringer later.

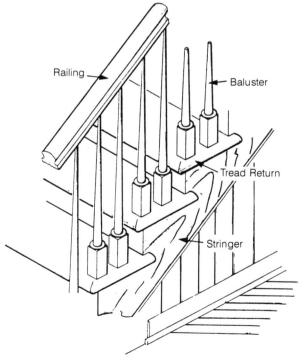

Fig. 8-16. Finish off a stairway with stock balusters and railings.

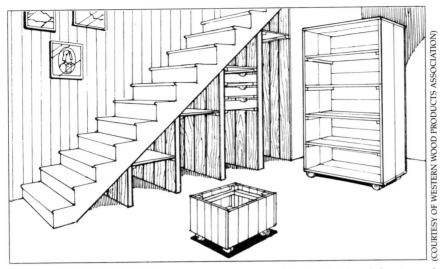

(COURTESY OF WESTERN WOOD PRODUCTS ASSOCIATION)

Fig. 8-17. An innovative method for using a combination of fixed and rolling shelves to maximize the storage under a set of basement stairs.

Fig. 8-18. A room storage closet is incorporated into the wall where the landing turns.

9

Finishing the Interior

WITH THE ROOMS ENCLOSED AND ALL THE STRUCTURAL WORK BEHIND YOU, NOW is the time to let the new space reflect a little of you. Here is where you finish the interior, select the colors and textures, define the space, and create a look that is all your own.

Attics and basements have a very separate feeling from the rest of the house, which might or might not be to your liking. On the one hand, you have the opportunity to indulge your fantasies and invent a look and style in that area that is unique, regardless of the decor of the rest of the house. On the other hand, that feeling of separateness might be what you're trying to avoid, seeking instead to establish a cohesiveness between these rather isolated areas and the rest of the house.

Garages are usually treated a little differently. In most instances, the separating wall between the house and the garage has been completely or substantially removed. The new area is very visible and, as a result, very much a part of the original living areas.

Sometimes, the room's use or its occupants will dictate the style. A game room, for example, might have its look already established by virtue of the massive dark-oak pool table you purchased. A home office for an independent businesswoman might have a uniquely feminine touch in the desk, chairs, or even some of the office machinery.

Try and establish what you intend to do with the rooms in the early stages of construction. Some items, like bay windows and certain door and window styles, need to be incorporated into the initial construction phases.

Other things, like moldings or wallcoverings, become part of the finishing touches. The sooner you establish the look you're trying to achieve, the better. It will simplify the color and material selection as well as furniture selection and the choice of the room's appointments. You'll save time, money, and a lot of frustration.

DRYWALL

In all likelihood, much or perhaps all of the interior of your attic, basement, or garage renovation will be covered with *gypsum wallboard*. Wallboard, known collectively as *drywall* or by the common trade name *Sheetrock*, is the most popular wall and ceiling covering material in use today (FIG. 9-1). It is versatile, easy to install, and with a little patience and practice, easy to finish and decorate.

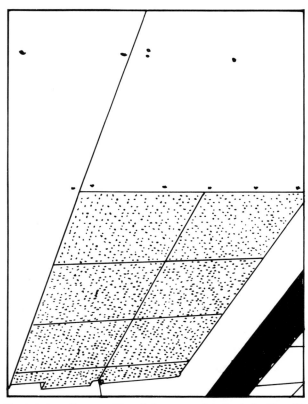

Fig. 9-1. Install new wallboard sheets over deteriorated ceiling tiles.

If you intend to use wallboard, try and have it delivered to the job site in advance. The sheets are heavy and awkward, especially if you have to negotiate them up or down a narrow set of stairs. Many companies will deliver the materials to your site for a nominal charge, which is well worth it. Some suppliers even have loading equipment that can place the materials on a second- or third-story floor (FIG. 9-2), saving you a tremendous amount of time-consuming labor.

Fig. 9-2. A hydraulic lift truck can deliver drywall sheets to a second-story remodeling project.

Cutting the Panels

Wallboard panels are most often cut using a razor knife and straightedge. Measure and mark the panel, place the straightedge along the marks, then use the knife to score the face of the sheet. Use a sharp knife blade and cut through the face paper and slightly into the panel's gypsum core. (Change blades often while you work because the gypsum will build up and dull the edge.) Support the larger portion of the panel near the score line, then press down on the smaller piece to snap the panel along the cut. Finally, cut the back paper to separate the pieces.

The panels can also be cut with a wide-toothed saw blade, either using a handsaw or an electric reciprocating saw. While sawing is much slower work than scoring and snapping for the main panel cuts, it is the common method of making cutouts for windows, doors, electrical outlets, and similar openings. For best results and fastest cutting with a minimum of blade clogging, purchase a saw designed specifically for cutting gypsum wallboard.

Installation Procedures

The panels can be installed either vertically or horizontally (FIG. 9-3), and the choice is made to minimize the number of seams that have to be finished.

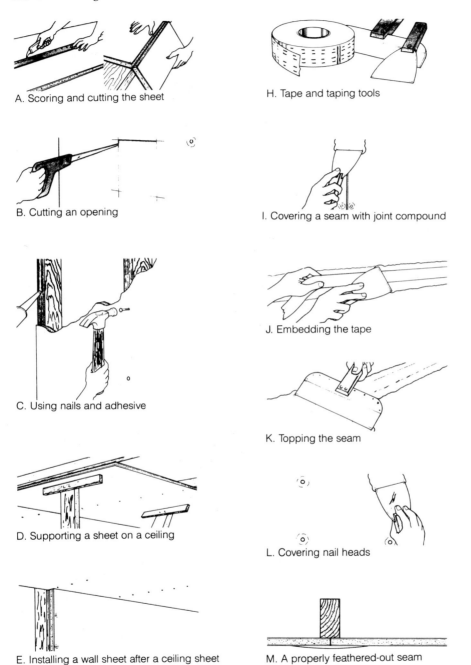

A. Scoring and cutting the sheet

H. Tape and taping tools

B. Cutting an opening

I. Covering a seam with joint compound

C. Using nails and adhesive

J. Embedding the tape

K. Topping the seam

D. Supporting a sheet on a ceiling

L. Covering nail heads

E. Installing a wall sheet after a ceiling sheet

M. A properly feathered-out seam

Fig. 9-3. The step-by-step installation of gypsum wallboard. (COURTESY OF GEORGIA-PACIFIC CORPORATION)

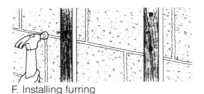

F. Installing furring

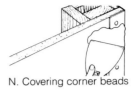

N. Covering corner beads

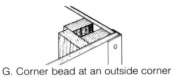

G. Corner bead at an outside corner

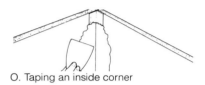

O. Taping an inside corner

Fig. 9-3. Cont. (COURTESY OF GEORGIA-PACIFIC CORPORATION)

The most common sheet size is 4 feet × 8 feet, but 4-foot-×-12-foot sheets are also commonly available and are, again, used to minimize the number of seams.

Install the sheets so that the tapered edges butt against each other whenever possible, simplifying the taping and finishing procedure. Also, be certain that the seams in the sheets fall over a stud or joist to properly support the joint.

Attach the panels using nails or screws. If nailing, select cup-headed drywall nails or ring-shank nails, which are designed for maximum holding power and a minimum of finishing effort. Use a drywall hammer or a regular hammer with a *crowned* (slightly rounded) face. Drive the nail in so that the hammer head *dimples* the face of the panel, creating a small concave recess for the nail head that allows it to be finished over and concealed. Be certain that you do not drive the nail head all the way through the paper face.

If you are using screws, select drywall screws that are specifically designed for this application. They have a sharp, self-starting point, course threads for good holding power and rapid installation, and a specially designed head that recesses into the paper without tearing through it. Use a drywall screwdriver, which you can buy or rent, to install the screws. They are fast, powerful, and have a built-in stop mechanism that countersinks the screw to the proper depth.

There are a variety of prefabricated metal corners, called *corner bead*, that simplify the finishing of outside corners. Install the corner bead over the wallboard corner joint, align it so that it is visually vertical and not pulled over to one side or the other, and secure it with nails or screws approximately every 8 inches.

Finishing the Seams

The seams are concealed using a paper or mesh tape and two or more layers of a special wallboard cement, called *joint compound*. The finishing process is not particularly difficult, although the techniques require some time and patience to master. If this is the first time you've worked with wallboard, you might want to begin in a closet or other semiconcealed area to practice your technique.

First, tape the seams. Using a 6-inch taping knife, apply a layer of joint compound to the seam. Place a length of tape over the compound, then use your taping knife to embed the tape and draw off the excess cement. The tape should still be slightly visible when you're done, but should be firmly embedded and free of wrinkles, bubbles, or loose areas.

Inside corners are also finished using the tape and joint compound. Apply a layer of compound to each side of the corner, fold the tape along the preformed crease in the middle, then apply it to the corner and embed it into the joint compound with your knife.

If you used a corner bead over the outside corners, finish them using joint compound only without tape. Rest one side of your taping knife on the raised corner bead and the side on the wall, then draw the knife down the wall. This will leave a layer of joint compound that feathers out from the metal bead onto the wall.

Tape all of the seams and corners and apply a first layer of joint compound to all the outside corners. Allow the compound to dry for at least 24 hours.

For the second coat of joint compound, called the *topping coat*, you will use a wider drywall knife. Most contractors prefer a 12-inch wide blade for this operation, but others use 8-, 10-, or even 14-inch blades, depending on personal preference. Using the wider knife, apply a second coat of compound over the first, completely concealing the tape and allowing the compound to feather out onto the wall on either side of the seam. Cover the outside corners a second time in the same manner; use the 6-inch blade to apply a second coat to the inside corners.

Allow the second coat to dry, then lightly sand it to remove the rough spots. Depending on the quality of the second coat and the type of texturing or other finish coat you want to apply, a third topping coat might be needed.

If you intend to paint the wallboard, you can obtain a very nice look by first applying texturing to the face of the panels (FIGS. 9-4 and 9-5). This can be done with regular or thinned joint compound, or any one of a variety of texturing materials available at your drywall or building materials supplier. The texture can be applied using a trowel, brush, broom, sponge, air-powered sprayer, or a variety of other means. Consult with your supplier for more details on the proper materials and application methods for the look you'd like to achieve.

Fig. 9-4. A taped and topped ceiling ready for texturing. The plastic sheeting protects the stairway during the texture-spraying operation.

(COURTESY OF GEORGIA-PACIFIC CORPORATION)

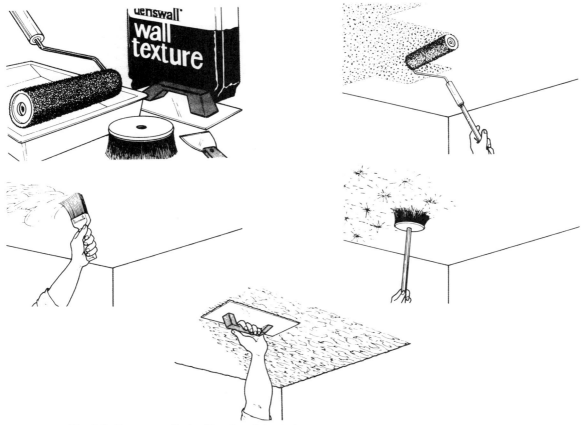

Fig. 9-5. Common methods of hand-applying texture. (COURTESY OF GEORGIA-PACIFIC CORPORATION)

PANELING

As an alternative to wallboard, you might consider covering the walls with any one of the wide variety of paneling materials available. Paneling offers a much different look than painted drywall, and many of the paneling products you can choose from are prefinished, speeding and simplifying the installation.

Sheet Paneling

The simplest of the paneling materials are the sheet panels, which are mostly prefinished and available in 4-×-8- foot or 4-×-9-foot panels for fast installation. Thicker panels of $^1/_2$ inch or more can be applied directly to the studs, while thinner panels need to be applied over drywall.

You can select from a wide variety of panels, depending on your needs, tastes, and budget. Some panels are constructed from real wood veneers, including exotic woods such as ebony and teak, that have been carefully selected, matched, stained, and finished. Lesser-expensive panels are made from *hardboard* (sawdust and wood by-products that are mixed with adhesive and formed into sheets). The panels are pressed and molded to simulate wood grain and are then stained and finished. Least expensive of all are panels covered with a photoengraved paper that tries as best it can to simulate something that looks like real wood.

In addition to the wood look, you can purchase panels that look like wallpapered gypsum board. The panels, again in 4-×-8-foot sheets, are available in a wide variety of face designs and colors to match almost any decor.

Bring the panels onto the job site early and allow them to adjust to the temperature and humidity conditions. This will minimize expansion and warpage after installation. Install the panels with nails, adhesive, or for best results, a combination of both. Colored nails are available to match or blend with almost any paneling color.

The seams between sheets must fall over a stud or other support for proper backing of the joint. Most panels are grooved at regular intervals on the face, so the seams blend in with the rest of the groove lines. Matching moldings are available to cover the seams if desired, along with the joints at the ceiling, floor, or corners, and around windows and doors.

Wood Paneling Strips

Beautiful results can be obtained with wood paneling strips (FIG. 9-6). Though more expensive and more time-consuming to install than the sheet panels, these are actual boards, with all the beauty and variations found in any real wood.

The boards are available in a variety of wood types, sizes, and edge treatments, including tongue-and-groove, beveled edge, and V-groove (FIG. 9-7). Some types are prefinished and ready for installation, although most

Fig. 9-6. Wood paneling strips applied to a vaulted attic ceiling.

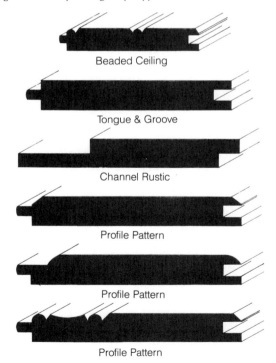

Beaded Ceiling

Tongue & Groove

Channel Rustic

Profile Pattern

Profile Pattern

Profile Pattern

Fig. 9-7. Common paneling strip configurations. (COURTESY OF WESTERN WOOD PRODUCTS ASSOCIATION)

require staining and sealing on-site. Once again, the material should be stored at the job as far in advance as possible.

Installation is with finish nails, adhesive, or a combination. If you have a lot of material to install, you might want to consider renting an air compressor and a finish-nail air gun. With most types of wood paneling strips, the boards can be installed vertically (although this requires additional blocking on 24-inch centers between the studs to give you something to nail to), horizontally, or for variety and visual appeal, at an angle (FIG. 9-8). Many people choose to do a combination of two or three of these patterns, using some strips as a border around the room.

MOLDINGS

Don't overlook the use of moldings to really dress up a room and give it your unique touch! There are dozens of stock molding patterns that are readily available at your lumber dealer (FIG. 9-9), and they can be used throughout the room in a variety of ways. You can even combine two or more patterns to create larger moldings for dramatic effect or to simulate the heavy moldings of the past.

Some areas where you might consider moldings would be at the joint between the wall and the ceiling. Moldings here can also help hide a difficult joint of camouflage obstructions. Heavy moldings at the wall/floor joint—or a combination of 1 × 4s or 1 × 6s with smaller moldings—can cover another difficult joint area. Add molding around doors and windows or replace smaller, less decorative molding. As a chair rail, molding can break up tall walls or separate two different wall coverings. At any joint or obstacle, molding can be a creative disguise to help you overcome what might otherwise be an eyesore.

CEILING TREATMENTS

Ceilings can be covered with drywall, following the same techniques used for the walls. Drywall jacks can be rented inexpensively to help you support and position the sheets against the ceiling joists, or you can construct simple wooden props to help set the sheets in place.

In many cases, however, particularly in the basement, protrusions and obstacles hang below the joists, making it impossible to drywall the ceiling without first moving or boxing around these items to create a smooth surface for application of the sheets. Drywalling the ceiling might be completely impossible, or it might involve so much additional work as to be impractical. The best solution for the remodeler at this point is to use a suspended ceiling.

Vertical Paneling

Horizontal Paneling

Diagonal Paneling

Flush Wall Surfaces

Herringbone Paneling

Board and Batten
and Board on Board

Multi-level Board on Board

Fig. 9-8. Some of the many ways to apply wood paneling strips to walls and ceilings. (COURTESY OF WESTERN WOOD PRODUCTS ASSOCIATION)

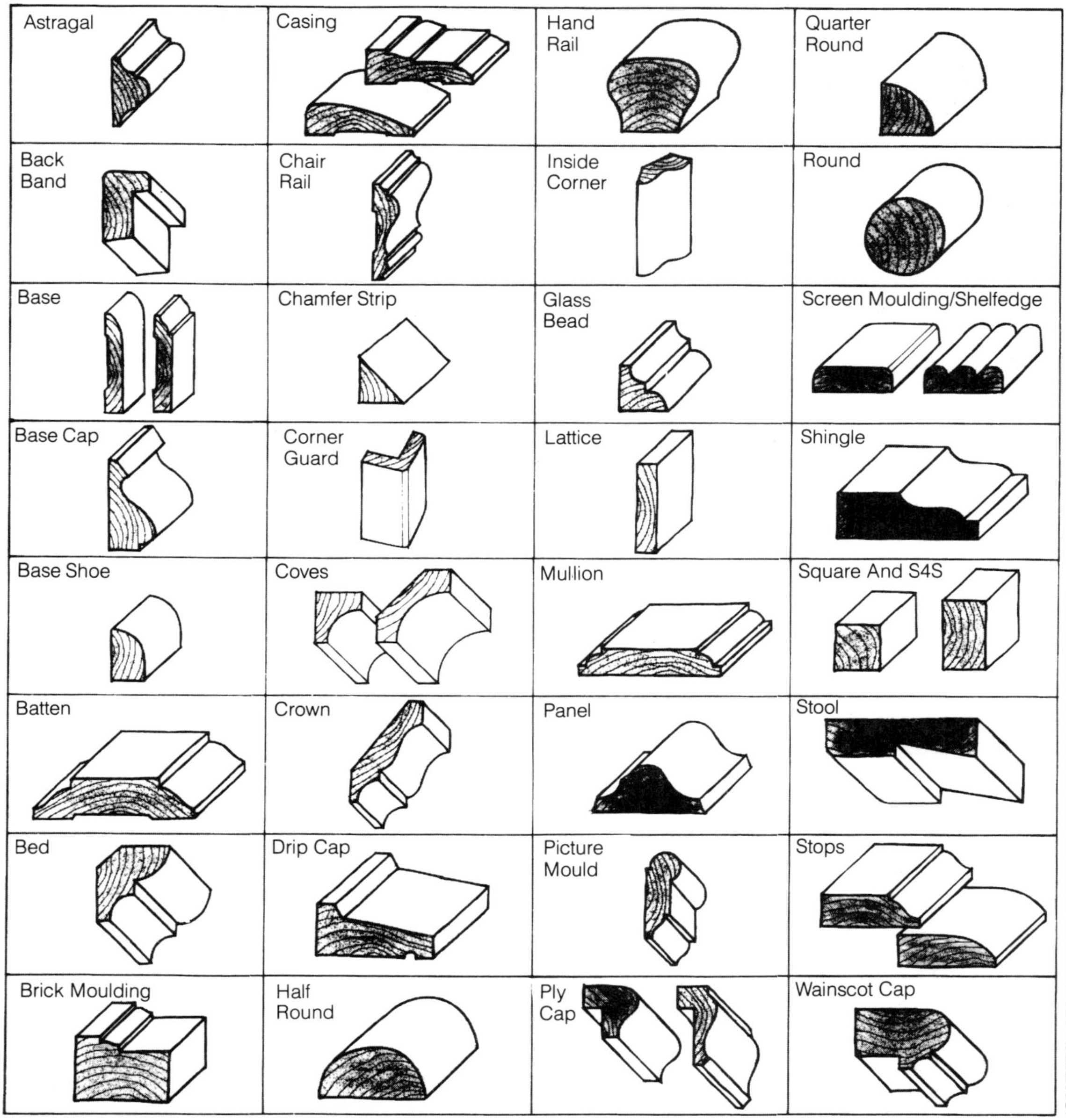

Astragal	Casing	Hand Rail	Quarter Round
Back Band	Chair Rail	Inside Corner	Round
Base	Chamfer Strip	Glass Bead	Screen Moulding/Shelfedge
Base Cap	Corner Guard	Lattice	Shingle
Base Shoe	Coves	Mullion	Square And S4S
Batten	Crown	Panel	Stool
Bed	Drip Cap	Picture Mould	Stops
Brick Moulding	Half Round	Ply Cap	Wainscot Cap

Fig. 9-9. A few of the dozens of commonly available molding patterns.

(COURTESY OF MOULDING AND MILLWORK PRODUCERS ASSOCIATION)

Suspended Ceiling Systems

As the name implies, a suspended ceiling is actually hung from the structural framework of the old ceiling. A gridwork is created and hung by wires, then decorative panels—and lights, if desired—are installed in the grid. By suspending the grid, you are able to drop it below the pipes, ducts, and all the rest of the maze on the ceiling, but at the same time, the lift-out panels still provide access to everything should servicing or repair be necessary.

Installation begins by attaching an L-shaped channel to the walls (FIG. 9-10). Establish a height on the wall that is below any obstructions, yet high enough to meet the minimum head-room standards. Mark this height at several locations, then use a chalk line to snap a level line on the wall around the entire room. Attach the wall channel to the studs with nails or screws.

(COURTESY OF ARMSTRONG)

Fig. 9-10. Installing the wall track for a suspended ceiling system.

Temporarily lay out part of the grid on the floor to establish how the grid pieces will run and where you will need to cut the panels. Most panels are 2 feet × 4 feet, so you lay the main runners of the grid on 2-foot centers, with cross-grids on 4-foot centers. For best appearance, most contractors lay out the system with the 4-foot dimensions of the grid running parallel with the long dimension of the room.

You can begiin the layout from one wall and leave all your cuts to go against the opposite wall, or you can split the cuts on two opposite walls.

> *Example*: If the room is 23 feet wide, you could begin from one wall with 11-×-2-foot-wide panels, and end up with a 1-foot panel at the opposite wall. Or, you could start with a 6-inch panel, lay 11-×-2-foot panels, then finish with another 6-inch piece.

Following the main grid layout you've selected, install eyebolts or special grid suspension hooks (available where you buy the rest of the system) into the ceiling framing. Fasten the hooks over the main grid runners and on 4-foot centers.

Mark the wall channel on two opposite walls where the first main runner will begin, and stretch a string between those points. Lay one end of the main runner in the wall channel, then begin working your way across the room, suspending the channel with wire from the ceiling hooks as you go (FIG. 9-11). The string will act as a guide to keep the grid pieces level. Interlock additional pieces by snapping them into place until you reach the opposite wall, then cut the last piece to length with snips or a hacksaw and rest it on the wall channel.

(COURTESY OF ARMSTRONG)

Fig. 9-11. *Suspending the main runners from wires. Note the eyebolts screwed into the ceiling joists.*

Move the string down 2 feet and install the next main runner. Continue in this manner until all the main runners of the grid have been installed. Double-check that the system is level and that all the support wires are in place.

Install the cross-runners of the grid next (FIG. 9-12). These runners are all 2 feet long and simply snap into slots in the main runners on 4-foot centers. Cut the crosspieces as needed when you reach the side walls and rest the cut ends in the wall channels.

The final step is to simply drop the panels into the grid (FIG. 9-13). Use a razor knife or an electric saw with a plywood blade to cut panels to drop into the smaller sections of the grid. If desired, 2-foot-×-4-foot fluorescent light boxes are available that also drop right into the grid system.

(COURTESY OF ARMSTRONG)

Fig. 9-12. Installing the cross-tracks.

Other Ceiling Options

In addition to the suspended ceiling, other decorative treatments are available for the ceiling. Acoustic tiles, which help absorb reflected sound, are another common alternative. They are available in a variety of sizes starting at 1-foot-×-1-foot squares or as strips that resemble individual planks.

(COURTESY OF ARMSTRONG)

Fig. 9-13. Dropping the ceiling panels into the grid system.

Tiles such as these require a solid surface to attach to, just as drywall panels would. First, a layout is established, again taking into consideration where you want the cut tiles to fall at the edges of the room for best appearance. Most tiles can be attached with adhesive directly to the old drywall or plaster ceiling if it is in reasonably good condition.

If the old ceiling is in bad shape, or if it is just bare joists, furring strips of 1-×-2 lumber can be installed (FIG. 9-14). Install the furring perpendicular to the joists, following the layout you established earlier, and nail the strips directly to the ceiling. Use shims as necessary to keep the furring level. The ceiling tiles are then installed one at a time, interlocking the edges and stapling them to the furring.

Some manufacturers also offer a simple prefabricated grid system. The grid is attached to the ceiling (FIG. 9-15). The special clips are used to interlock the tiles and attach them to the grid channels (FIG. 9-16). Although a little

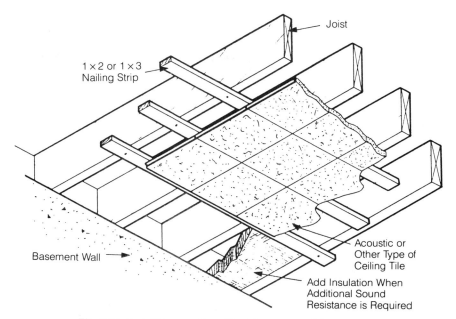

Joist

1 × 2 or 1 × 3
Nailing Strip

Basement Wall

Acoustic or
Other Type of
Ceiling Tile

Add Insulation When
Additional Sound
Resistance is Required

Fig. 9-14. Installing acoustic ceiling tiles over wood furring strips.

(COURTESY OF ARMSTRONG)

Fig. 9-15. Installing a premanufactured ceiling track system.

Fig. 9-16. Attaching the interlocking ceiling panels to the ceiling tracks.

(COURTESY OF ARMSTRONG)

more expensive, installation is faster and cleaner, and the resulting ceiling is usually a little more uniform in appearance.

FLOOR COVERINGS

You can choose between a wide variety of finished floor coverings for your newly remodeled areas, either to match existing flooring in the rest of the house or to create a new look in these rooms. Options include wall-to-wall carpeting, linoleum, floor tiles, ceramic tile, or squares or strips of hardwood.

In the attic, where you are installing the floor covering over a wood subfloor, you can use any material you'd like with no special preparations. If the subfloor is rough, you should plan on first installing an underlayment of $3/8$-inch particleboard or similar material to give you a smooth surface to work on (FIG. 9-17).

(COURTESY OF LOUISIANA-PACIFIC CORPORATION)

Fig. 9-17. Using mastic to install underlayment over the subflooring in a new bathroom.

In the basement or garage, where the floor covering will be laid over a concrete slab, a few precautions against moisture are necessary (FIGS. 9-18 and 9-19). If the existing slab is in poor condition, repair and level it before installing the floor covering. You can install a new concrete slab directly over the old one using a binder material for best adhesion. This second slab typically needs to be a minimum of 2 to 3 inches thick, which might present a problem in some instances. The best alternative is to have a contractor come in and level the floor with one of the new liquid mortar or gypsum/concrete mixtures that are now available just for this purpose. This creates a smooth, hard, level floor and requires only about $3/4$ to 1 inch of thickness.

To install linoleum, floor tile, or ceramic tile, use a waterproof mastic to adhere the flooring directly to the concrete. Install carpeting or hardwood flooring over a vapor barrier of plastic sheeting to prevent moisture in the concrete from working its way up and ruining the flooring.

Step One: Seal concrete slab with primer and spread mastic.

Step Two: Cover mastic with polyethylene sheet to form moisture barrier.

Step Three: Lay your 2″ × 4″ pressure treated sleepers along chalk lines, leaving a ¹/₂″ gap between the end of the sleeper and the wall.

Step Four: Nail plywood subfloor in place over wood sleepers.

Fig. 9-18. *Installing a vapor barrier and sleepers over a concrete slab floor prior to the installation of new plywood subflooring.* (COURTESY OF GEORGIA-PACIFIC CORPORATION)

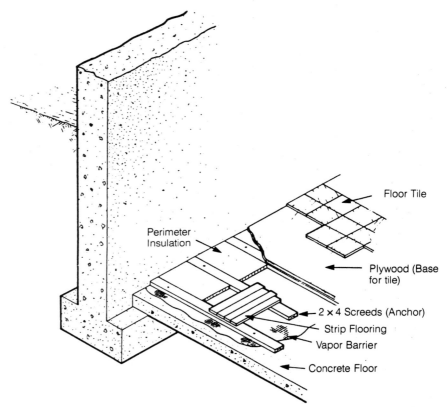

Floor Tile

Perimeter Insulation

Plywood (Base for tile)

2 x 4 Screeds (Anchor)

Strip Flooring

Vapor Barrier

Concrete Floor

Fig. 9-19. Two other methods of furring and insulating a concrete floor prior to installation of the finished flooring materials.

Appendix A
Conversions,
Tables, and Weights

CONVERSION TABLES

Multiply	By	To Obtain
Acres	43,560	Square feet
Acre-feet	43,560	Cubic feet
Acre-feet	325,851	Gallons
Atmospheres	76	Centimeters of mercury
Atmospheres	29.92	Inches of mercury
Atmospheres	33.90	Feet of water
Atmospheres	14.70	Pounds/square inch
Btu/hour	0.2931	Watts
Btu/minute	0.02356	Horsepower
Btu/minute	60	Btu/hour
Btu/minute	0.01757	Kilowatts
Btu/minute	17.57	Watts
Centimeters	0.3937	Inches
Centimeters of mercury	0.01316	Atmospheres
Centimeters of mercury	0.4461	Feet of water
Centimeters of mercury	27.85	Pounds/square foot
Centimeters of mercury	0.1934	Pounds/square inch
Cubic centimeters	0.06102	Cubic inches
Cubic feet	1728	Cubic inches
Cubic feet	0.02832	Cubic meters
Cubic feet	0.03704	Cubic yards
Cubic feet	7.48052	Gallons
Cubic feet	28.32	Liters
Cubic feet	29.92	Quarts (liquid)
Cubic feet/minute	472	Cubic centimeters/second
Cubic feet/minute	0.1274	Gallons/second

Multiply	By	To Obtain
Cubic feet/minute	62.43	Pounds of water/minute
Cubic feet/second	0.646317	Million gallons/day
Cubic feet/second	448.831	Gallons/minute
Cubic inches	16.39	Cubic centimeters
Cubic inches	0.01639	Liters
Cubic meters	264.2	Gallons (U.S. liquid)
Cubic yards	27	Cubic feet
Cubic yards	46,656	Cubic inches
Degrees Centigrade + 273	1	Absolute temp (C)
Degrees Centigrade + 17.28	1.8	Degrees Fahrenheit
Degrees Fahrenheit + 460	1	Absolute temp (F)
Degrees Fahrenheit − 32	.5556	Degrees Centigrade
Feet	30.48	Centimeters
Feet	12	Inches
Feet	0.3048	Meters
Feet	304.8	Millimeters
Feet of water	0.02950	Atmospheres
Feet of water	0.8826	Inches of mercury
Feet of water	62.43	Pounds/square foot
Feet of water	0.4335	Pounds/square inch
Feet/minute	0.01667	Feet/second
Feet/minute	0.01136	Miles/hour
Feet/second	0.6818	Miles/hour
Feet/second	0.01136	Miles/minute
Foot-pounds/minute	2.260×10^{-5}	Kilowatts
Foot-pounds/second	1.356×10^{-3}	Kilowatts
Gallons	3785	Cubic centimeters
Gallons	0.1337	Cubic feet
Gallons	231	Cubic inches
Gallons	3.785	Liters
Gallons	4	Quarts (dry)
Gallons of water	8.3453	Pounds of water
Gallons/minute	0.002228	Cubic feet/second
Gallons/minute	8.0208	Cubic feet/hour
Gallons of water/minute	6.0086	Tons of water/24 hours
Horsepower	745.7	Watts
Horsepower hours	0.7457	Kilowatt hours
Inches	2.540	Centimeters
Inches of mercury	0.03342	Atmospheres
Inches of mercury	1.133	Feet of water
Inches of mercury	0.4912	Pounds/square foot
Inches of water	0.002458	Atmospheres
Inches of water	0.07355	Inches of mercury
Inches of water	5.202	Pounds/square foot
Inches of water	0.03613	Pounds/square inch
Kilograms	2.205	Pounds
Kilograms	1.102×10^{-3}	Tons
Kilometers	0.6214	Miles
Kilometers/hour	0.6214	Miles/hour
Kilowatts	1.341	Horsepower
Kilowatt hours	3,413	Btus
Kilowatt hours	2.655×10^{6}	Foot pounds
Liters	1,000	Cubic centimeters
Liters	0.03531	Cubic feet
Liters	61.02	Cubic inches
Liters	0.2642	Gallons
Meters	3.281	Feet

Multiply	By	To Obtain
Meters	39.37	Inches
Meters	1.094	Yards
Meters/second	3.281	Feet/second
Meters/second	2.237	Miles/hour
Miles	5,280	Feet
Miles	1.609	Kilometers
Miles/hour	1.467	Feet/second
Miles/hour	26.82	Meters/minute
Millimeters	0.1	Centimeters
Millimeters	0.03937	Inches
Million gallons/day	1.54723	Cubic feet/second
Ounces (fluid)	0.02957	Liters
Pints (liquid)	473.2	Cubic centimeters
Pounds	0.4536	Kilograms
Pounds of water	0.01602	Cubic feet
Pounds of water	27.68	Cubic inches
Pounds of water	0.1198	Gallons
Pounds/cubic inch	1,728	Pounds/cubic foot
Pounds/square foot	0.01602	Feet of water
Pounds/square inch	0.06804	Atmospheres
Pounds/square inch	2.307	Feet of water
Pounds/square inch	2.036	Inches of mercury
Pounds/square inch	6,895	Pascals
Quarts (dry)	67.20	Cubic inches
Quarts (liquid)	57.75	Cubic inches
Quarts (liquid)	0.9463	Liters
Square feet	144	Square inches
Square inches	645.2	Square millimeters
Square meters	1,550	Square inches
Square miles	640	Acres
Square millimeters	1.550×10^{-3}	Square inches
Square yards	9	Square feet
Square yards	1,296	Square inches
Tons	2,000	Pounds
Watts	3.4129	Btu/hour
Watts	0.05688	Btu/minute
Watts	0.7378	Foot pounds/second
Watts	1.341×10^{-3}	Horsepower
Yards	3	Feet
Yards	36	Inches

WEIGHTS AND MEASURES

Metric System

Length

Unit			Metric Equivalent			U.S. Equivalent	
millimeter	(mm)	=	0.001	meter	=	0.03937	inch
centimeter	(cm)	=	0.01	meter	=	0.3937	inch
decimeter	(dm)	=	0.1	meter	=	3.937	inches
METER	(m)	=	1.0	meter	=	39.37	inches
dekameter	(dkm)	=	10.0	meters	=	10.93	yards
hectometer	(hm)	=	100.0	meters	=	328.08	feet
kilometer	(km)	=	1000.0	meters	=	0.6214	mile

Weight or Mass

Unit			Metric Equivalent			U.S. Equivalent	
milligram	(mg)	=	0.001	gram	=	0.0154	grain
centigram	(cg)	=	0.01	gram	=	0.1543	grain
decigram	(dg)	=	0.1	gram	=	1.543	grains
GRAM	(g)	=	1.0	gram	=	15.43	grains
dekagram	(dkg)	=	10.0	grams	=	0.3527	ounce avoirdupois
hectogram	(hg)	=	100.0	grams	=	3.527	ounces avoirdupois
kilogram	(kg)	=	1000.0	grams	=	2.2	pounds avoirdupois

Capacity

Unit			Metric Equivalent			U.S. Equivalent	
milliliter	(ml)	=	0.001	liter	=	0.034	fluid ounce
centiliter	(cl)	=	0.01	liter	=	0.338	fluid ounce
deciliter	(dl)	=	0.1	liter	=	3.38	fluid ounces
LITER	(l)	=	1.0	liter	=	1.05	liquid quarts
dekaliter	(dkl)	=	10.0	liters	=	0.284	bushel
hectoliter	(hl)	=	100.0	liters	=	2.837	bushels
kiloliter	(kl)	=	1000.0	liters	=	264.18	gallons

Area

Unit			Metric Equivalent			U.S. Equivalent	
square millimeter	(mm^2)	=	0.000001	centare	=	0.00155	square inch
square centimeter	(cm^2)	=	0.0001	centare	=	0.155	square inch
square decimeter	(dm^2)	=	0.01	centare	=	15.5	square inches
CENTARE *also*	(ca)	=	1.0	centare	=	10.76	square feet
square meter	(m^2)						
are *also*	(a)	=	100.0	centares	=	0.0247	acre
square dekameter	(dkm^2)						
hectare *also*	(ha)	=	10,000.0	centares	=	2.47	acres
square hectometer	(hm^2)						
square kilometer	(km^2)	=	1,000,000.0	centares	=	0.386	square mile

Volume

Unit			Metric Equivalent			U.S. Equivalent	
cubic millimeter	(mm^3)	=	0.001	cubic centimeter	=	0.016	minim
cubic centimeter	(cc, cm^3)	=	0.001	cubic decimeter	=	0.061	cubic inch
cubic decimeter	(dm^3)	=	0.001	cubic meter	=	61.023	cubic inches
STERE *also*	(s)	=	1.0	cubic meter	=	1.308	cubic yards
cubic meter	(m^3)						
cubic dekameter	(dkm^3)	=	1000.0	cubic meters	=	1307.943	cubic yards
cubic hectometer	(hm^3)	=	1,000,000.0	cubic meters	=	1,307,942.8	cubic yards
cubic kilometer	(km^3)	=	1,000,000,000.0	cubic meters	=	0.25	cubic mile

U.S. System

Liquid Measure

4	gills	=	1 pint (pt.)
2	pints	=	1 quart (qt.)
4	quarts	=	1 gallon (gal.)
31.5	gallons	=	1 barrel (bbl.)
2	barrels	=	1 hogshead
60	minims	=	1 fluid dram (fl. dr.)

Linear Measure

1	mil	=	0.001 inch (in.)
12	inches	=	1 foot (ft.)
3	feet	=	1 yard (yd.)
6	feet	=	1 fathom
5.5	yards	=	1 rod (rd.)
40	rods	=	1 furlong

Liquid Measure

8	fluid drams	=	1 fluid ounce (fl. oz.)
16	fluid ounces	=	1 pint

Square Measure

144	square inches (sq. in.)	=	1 square foot (sq. ft.)
9	square feet	=	1 square yard (sq. yd.)
30.25	square yards	=	1 square rod (sq. rd.)
160	square rods	=	1 acre (A.)
640	acres	=	1 square mile (sq. mi.)

Avoirdupois Weight

27.34	grains (gr.)	=	1 dram (dr. av.)
16	drams	=	1 ounce (oz. av.)
16	ounces	=	1 pound (lb. av.)
2000	pounds	=	1 short ton (sh. tn.)
2240	pounds	=	1 long ton (l. tn.)

Cubic Measure

144	cubic inches (cu. in.)	=	1 board foot (bd. ft.)
1728	cubic inches	=	1 cubic foot (cu. ft.)
27	cubic feet	=	1 cubic yard (cu. yd.)
128	cubic feet	=	1 cord (cd.)

Linear Measure

5280	feet	=	1 mile (mi.)
1760	yards	=	1 mile

Apothecaries' Weight

20	grains (gr.)	=	1 scruple
3	scruples	=	1 dram (dr.)
8	drams	=	1 ounce (oz.)
12	ounces	=	1 pound (lb.)

Troy Weight

24	grains	=	1 pennyweight (dwt.)
20	pennyweight	=	1 ounce (oz. t.)
12	ounces	=	1 pound (lb. t.)

Dry Measure

2	pints	=	1 quart (qt.)
8	quarts	=	1 peck (pk.)
4	pecks	=	1 bushel (bu.)
3.28	bushels	=	1 barrel (bbl.)

WEIGHTS OF COMMON MATERIALS

Earth	Weight (lb/cu ft)
Clay, dry	63
Clay, damp	110
Clay and gravel, dry	100
Earth, dry	76 to 95
Earth, moist	78 to 96
Earth, packed	100
Gravel	109
Mud	108 to 115
Sand and gravel, dry	90 to 120
Sand and gravel, wet	118 to 120

Lumber (15% MC)	Weight (lb/sq ft) Nominal Size		
	2"	3"	4"
Douglas fir	4.5	7.6	10.6
Hem-Fir	4.0	6.6	9.3
Englemann Spruce	3.1	5.1	7.2
Pine: Lodgepole, Ponderosa, Sugar	3.7	6.2	8.6
Western Cedar	3.3	5.5	7.7
Western Hemlock	4.0	6.6	9.3

Liquids	Weight (lb/cu ft)
Gasoline	42
Water, fresh	62.4
Water, ice	56
Water, sea	64

Masonry	Weight (lb/cu ft)
Cement, portland	90
Concrete, cinder	111
Concrete, slag	138
Concrete, sand and gravel	150
Brick, common	112
Brick, fire	144
Limestone	163
Sandstone	144

Metals	Weight (lb/cu ft)
Aluminum alloy, cast	171
Aluminum, cast	165
Brass, cast or rolled	526
Chromium	442
Copper, cast	540
Copper, rolled or wire	557
Gold	1,204
Iron, cast	450
Iron, wrought	480
Lead	710
Magnesium	109
Mercury	848
Silver	655
Steel, rolled	485
Steel, tool	470
Tin	455
Zinc	446

Roofing	Weight (lb/sq ft)
Built-up, 3 ply	1.5
Built-up, 3 ply w/gravel	5.5
Built-up, 5 ply	2.5
Built-up, 5 ply w/gravel	6.5
Roll Roofing	1.0
Galvanized steel, 2 1/2" and 3" corrugated, U.S. Standard Gauge, including laps:	
12 gauge	4.9
14 gauge	3.6
16 gauge	2.9
18 gauge	2.4
20 gauge	1.8
22 gauge	1.5
24 gauge	1.3
26 gauge	1.0
Shingles:	
Asphalt, 1/4"	2.0
Asbestos cement, 3/8"	4.0
Clay tile w/mortar	19.0 - 24.0
Slate, 1/4"	10.0
Spanish	19.0
Tile, 2"	12.0
Tile, 3"	20.0
Wood, 1"	3.0

Walls	Weight (lb/sq ft)
2 × 4 framing, bare:	
12" O.C.	1.3
16" O.C.	1.0
24" O.C.	0.7
Glass block, 4"	18.0
Glazed tile	18.0
Gypsum wallboard, 1/2"	2.5
Marble	15.0
Masonry, in 4" thickness:	
Brick	38.0
Concrete block	30.0
Concrete cinder block	20.0
Hollow clay tile, load-bearing	23.0
Hollow clay tile, non-bearing	18.0
Limestone	53.0
Stone	55.0
Terra cotta tile	25.0
Plaster, 1"	8.0
Plaster, 1" on wood lath	10.0
Plaster, 1" on metal lath	8.5
Porcelain-enameled steel	3.0
Stucco, 7/8"	10.0
Windows, glass frame and sash	8.0
Wood paneling, 1"	2.5

Wood	Weight (lb/cu ft)
Ash	41
Balsa	10
Cedar	29
Cork	16
Hickory	51
Maple	43
Oak, white	48
Pine, white	26
Pine, yellow	43
Poplar	31
Walnut, black	40

Miscellaneous	Weight (lb/cu ft)
Asbestos	175
Bakelite	79.5
Fiberglass, rigid	18
Glass	156
Glass, plate	161
Insulation, expanded polystyrene	2.4
Insulation, loose fiberglass	6
Pitch	69
Plexiglass	74.3
Tar	74

DECIMAL EQUIVALENTS

Fraction	Decimal	Fraction	Decimal
1/32	.03125	17/32	.53125
1/16	.0625	9/16	.5625
3/32	.09375	19/32	.59375
1/8	.125	5/8	.625
5/32	.15625	21/32	.65625
3/16	.1875	11/16	.6875
7/32	.21875	23/32	.71875
1/4	.250	3/4	.750
9/32	.28125	25/32	.78125
5/16	.3125	13/16	.8125
11/32	.34375	27/32	.84375
3/8	.375	7/8	.875
13/32	.40625	29/32	.90625
7/16	.4375	15/16	.9375
15/32	.46875	31/32	.96875
1/2	.500	1	1.000

APPROXIMATE R VALUES FOR COMMON BUILDING MATERIALS

Air	R-Value
Heat Flow Up:	
Air film (still air, inside wall)	0.61
3/4″ space	0.77
3 1/2″ space	0.84
Heat Flow Down:	
Air film (still air, inside wall)	0.92
3/4″ space	1.02
3 1/2″ space	1.22
Heat Flow Horizontal:	
Air film (still air, inside wall)	0.68
3/4″ space	0.94
3 1/2″ space	0.91
Outside air film, 7.5 mph wind	0.25
Outside air film, 15 mph wind	0.17

Building Boards	R-Value
Asbestos cement board, per inch	0.25
Asbestos cement board, 1/4″	0.07
Drywall, 3/8″	0.32
Drywall, 1/2″	0.45
Insulating board, 1/2″ drop-in ceiling tiles	1.25
Insulating board, 1/2″ sheathing	1.32
Hardboard, tempered, per inch	1.00
Particle board, medium density, per inch	1.06
Particle board, 5/8″ underlayment	0.82
Plywood, per inch	1.25
Plywood, 1/4″	0.31
Plywood, 3/8″	0.47
Plywood, 1/2″	0.63
Wood sheathing, plywood or wood panels, 3/4″	0.93

Flooring	R-Value
Asphalt tile, 3/16″	0.04
Carpet and fiber pad	2.08
Carpet and rubber pad	1.23
Ceramic tile, 1/4″	0.04
Cork tile, 1/8″	0.28
Linoleum	0.08
Hardwood strips, 5/8″	0.68

Masonry	R-Value
Brick, per inch	0.20
Cement mortar, per inch	0.20
Concrete, per inch	0.08
Concrete blocks, 8″	1.00
Gypsum plaster, perlite aggregate, per inch	0.67
Gypsum plaster, sand aggregate, per inch	0.18
Limestone or sandstone, per inch	0.08
Pumice blocks, 8″	2.00
Stucco, per inch	0.20

Paper	R-Value
Felt building paper	0.06
Felt flooring paper	0.06

Roofing	R-Value
Asbestos-cement shingles	0.21
Asphalt roll roofing	0.15
Asphalt shingles	0.44
Built-up roofing, 3/8″	0.33
Slate shingles, 1/2″	0.05
Wood shingles	0.94

Siding	R-Value
Aluminum or steel, hollow back	0.61
Asbestos-cement shingles	0.21
Asbestos roll	0.15
Wood, bevel siding, 1/2″ × 8″, lapped	0.81
Wood, bevel siding, 3/4″ × 10″, lapped	1.05
Wood, drop siding, 1″ × 8″	0.79
Wood, plywood, 3/8″	0.59
Wood siding shingles, 7 1/2″ exposure	0.87

Thermal Insulation	R-Value
Batts:	
Fiberglass, per inch	3.20
Mineral wool, per inch	3.50
Loose Fill:	
Cellulose, per inch	3.70
Fiberglass, per inch	2.20
Mineral wool	3.00
Perlite, expanded, per inch	2.70
Vermiculite, expanded, per inch	2.20

Thermal Insulation	R-Value
Wood shavings, per inch	2.20
Rigid:	
Polystyrene, expanded bead board, per inch	3.57
Polystyrene, extruded board, per inch	5.26
Polyurethane foam, per inch	6.25
Urea-formaldehyde foam, per inch	4.17

Wall Sections	R-Value
Standard frame wall, insulated	14.29
Standard frame wall, uninsulated	4.35

Windows	R-Value
Architectural glass	0.10
Double glass window, 1/4" air space	1.59
Double glass window, 1/2" air space	1.75
Single glass window	0.91
Single glass window, with storm, 1" to 4" air space	1.82

Wood	R-Value
Hardwood, per inch	0.91
Softwood, per inch	1.25
Softwood, 1 1/2"	1.89
Softwood, 3 1/2"	4.35

HEAT VALUE OF COMMON FIREPLACE FUELS

Fuel	Heat Value in Millions of Btus per cord	Btus per Pound
Ash, white	25.0	7,400
Beech	28.0	7,200
Birch, white	23.4	8,000
Cedar	16.5	7,900
Cherry	23.5	8,400
Chestnut	20.2	8,100
Coal, anthracite (hard)	—	15,000
Coal, bituminous (soft)	—	13,000
Elm, white	24.5	8,200
Fir, Douglas	21.4	8,600
Hickory	30.6	7,900
Maple, red	24.0	7,500
Maple, sugar	29.0	7,600
Oak, red	27.3	7,600
Oak, white	30.6	7,900
Pine, white	15.8	7,500
Sawdust logs	—	15,000
Spruce	17.5	8,300

Appendix B
Building Information

**RECOMMENDED NAILING SCHEDULE
FOR FRAMING AND SHEATHING**

Joining	Nailing Method	No.	Nails Size	Placement
Header to joist	End-nail	3	16d	
Joist to sill or girder	Toenail	2	10d or	
		3	8d	
Header and stringer joist to sill	Toenail		10d	16 in. on center
Bridging to joist	Toenail each end	2	8d	
Ledger strip to beam, 2 in. thick		3	16d	At each joist
Subfloor, boards:				
1 by 6 in. and smaller		2	8d	To each joist
1 by 8 in.		3	8d	To each joist
Subfloor, plywood:				
At edges			8d	6 in. on center
At intermediate joists			8d	8 in. on center
Subfloor (2 by 6 in., T&G) to joist or girder	Blind-nail (casing) and face-nail	2	16d	
Soleplate to stud, horizontal assembly	End-nail	2	16d	At each stud
Top plate to stud	End-nail	2	16d	
Stud to soleplate	Toenail	4	8d	
Soleplate to joist or blocking	Face-nail		16d	16-in. on center
Doubled studs	Face-nail, stagger		10d	16 in. on center
End stud of intersecting wall to exterior wall stud	Face-nail		16d	16 in. on center
Upper top plate to lower top plate	Face-nail		16d	16 in. on center
Upper top plate, laps and intersections	Face-nail	2	16d	
Continuous header, two pieces, each edge			12d	12 in. on center

Joining	Nailing Method	Nails No.	Nails Size	Placement
Ceiling joist to top wall plates	Toenail	3	8d	
Ceiling joist laps at partition	Face-nail	4	16d	
Rafter to top plate	Toenail	2	8d	
Rafter to ceiling joist	Face-nail	5	10d	
Rafter to valley or hip rafter	Toenail	3	10d	
Ridge board to rafter	End-nail	3	10d	
Rafter to rafter through ridge board	Toenail	4	8d	
	Edge-nail	1	10d	
Collar beam to rafter:				
2 in. member	Face-nail	2	12d	
1 in. member	Face-nail	3	8d	
1-in. diagonal let-in brace to each stud and plate				
(4 nails at top)		2	8d	
Built-up corner studs:				
Studs to blocking	Face-nail	2	10d	Each side
Intersecting stud to corner studs	Face-nail		16d	12 in. on center
Built-up girders and beams, three or more members	Face-nail		20d	32 in. on center, each side
Wall sheathing:				
1 by 8 in. or less, horizontal	Face-nail	2	8d	At each stud
1 by 6 in. or greater, diagonal	Face-nail	3	8d	At each stud
Wall sheathing, vertically applied plywood:				
3/8 in. and less thick	Face-nail		6d	6 in. edge
1/2 in. and over thick	Face-nail		8d	12 in. intermediate
Wall sheathing, vertically applied fiberboard:				
1/2 in. thick	Face-nail			1 1/2 in. roofing nail
				1 3/4 in. roofing nail
25/32 in. thick	Face-nail			3 in. edge and
				6 in. intermediate
Roof sheathing, boards, 4-, 6-, 8-in. width	Face-nail	2	8d	At each rafter
Roof sheathing, plywood:				
3/8 in. and less thick	Face-nail		6d }	6 in. edge and 12 in.
1/2 in. and over thick	Face-nail		8d }	intermediate

DEGREES OF SLOPE

Rise per 12″ of Run	Degrees of Slope	Rise per 12″ of Run	Degrees of Slope	Rise per 12″ of Run	Degrees of Slope	Rise per 12″ of Run	Degrees of Slope
1/2″	2 1/2″	6 1/2″	28 1/4	12 1/2″	46 1/4	18 1/2″	57
1″	4 1/2	7″	30 1/4	13″	47 1/4	19″	57 3/4
1 1/2″	7	7 1/2″	32	13 1/2″	48 1/2	19 1/2″	58 1/2
2″	9 1/2	8″	33 3/4	14″	49 1/2	20″	59
2 1/2″	11 3/4	8 1/2″	35 1/4	14 1/2″	50 1/2	20 1/2″	59 3/4
3″	14	9″	37	15″	51 1/2	21″	60 1/4
3 1/2″	16 1/4	9 1/2″	38 1/2	15 1/2″	52 1/4	21 1/2″	61
4″	18 1/2	10″	40	16″	53 1/4	22″	61 1/2
4 1/2″	20 1/2	10 1/2″	41 1/4	16 1/2″	54	22 1/2″	62
5″	22 1/2	11″	42 1/2	17″	54 3/4	23″	62 1/2
5 1/2″	24 1/2	11 1/2″	43 3/4	17 1/2″	55 1/2	23 1/2″	63
6″	26 1/2	12″	45	18″	56 1/4	24″	63 1/2

ESTIMATING NEEDS FOR DRY PREMIXED CONCRETE

Approximate Number of Bags To Use

Dimension in Feet: Width	Length	3″ Deep 60 lb bag	90 lb bag	4″ Deep 60 lb bag	90 lb bag
1	1	1/2	1/2	2/3	1/2
1	2	1	3/4	1 1/3	1
1	3	1 1/2	1 1/4	2	1 1/2
2	2	2	1 1/2	2 2/3	2
2	3	3	2 1/4	4	3
2	4	4	3	5 1/3	4
2	5	5	3 3/4	6 2/3	5
2	6	6	4 1/2	8	6
2	7	7	5 1/4	9 1/3	7
2	8	8	6	10 2/3	8
2	9	9	6 3/4	12	9
2	10	10	7 1/2	13 1/3	10
3	3	4 1/2	3 1/3	6	4 1/2
3	5	7 1/2	5 2/3	10	7 1/2
3	7	10 1/2	8	14	10 1/2

COMMON SOFTWOOD GRADES

WOOD	Top grade, best appearance, few if any defects	Slight defects, okay for most exposed work	General use for framing, outdoor use	Many defects, good for some rough usages
Redwood	Clear All Heart Clear	Select Heart Select	Constr. Heart Construction	Merchantable
Red Cedar	C and Better Finish	C Finish	Select Merchant. Construction	Standard
Douglas Fir	C and Better Finish	C Finish	Construction	Standard
Pine	C and Better 1 and 2 Clear Supreme	C Select Choice	Quality D Select	1-3 Dimension 1-5 Common Utility

TABLE OF BOARD MEASURE

NOMINAL SIZE OF PIECE	BOARD FEET CONTENT WHEN LENGTH IN FEET EQUALS											
	2	4	6	8	10	12	14	16	18	20	22	24
1×2	1/3	2/3	1	1 1/3	1 2/3	2	2 1/3	2 2/3	3	3 1/3	3 2/3	4
1×3	1/2	1	1 1/2	2	2 1/2	3	3 1/2	4	4 1/2	5	5 1/2	6
1×4	2/3	1 1/3	2	2 2/3	3 1/3	4	4 2/3	5 1/3	6	6 2/3	7 1/3	8
1×6	1	2	3	4	5	6	7	8	9	10	11	12
1×8	1 1/3	2 2/3	4	5 1/3	6 2/3	8	9 1/3	10 2/3	12	13 1/3	14 2/3	16
1×10	1 2/3	3 1/3	5	6 2/3	8 1/3	10	11 2/3	13 1/3	15	16 2/3	18 1/3	20
1×12	2	4	6	8	10	12	14	16	18	20	22	24
2×2	2/3	1 1/3	2	2 2/3	3 1/3	4	4 2/3	5 1/3	6	6 2/3	7 1/3	8
2×3	1	2	3	4	5	6	7	8	9	10	11	12
2×4	1 1/3	2 2/3	4	5 1/3	6 2/3	8	9 1/3	10 2/3	12	13 1/3	14 2/3	16
2×6	2	4	6	8	10	12	14	16	18	20	22	24
2×8	2 2/3	5 1/3	8	10 2/3	13 1/3	16	18 2/3	21 1/3	24	26 2/3	29 1/3	32
2×10	3 1/3	6 2/3	10	13 1/3	16 2/3	20	23 1/3	26 2/3	30	33 1/3	36 2/3	40
2×12	4	8	12	16	20	24	28	32	36	40	44	48
2×14	4 2/3	9 1/3	14	18 2/3	23 1/3	28	32 2/3	37 1/3	42	46 2/3	51 1/3	56
3×4	2	4	6	8	10	12	14	16	18	20	22	24
3×6	3	6	9	12	15	18	21	24	27	30	33	36
3×8	4	8	12	16	20	24	28	32	36	40	44	48
3×10	5	10	15	20	25	30	35	40	45	50	55	60
3×12	6	12	18	24	30	36	42	48	54	60	66	72
3×14	7	14	21	28	35	42	49	56	63	70	77	84
3×16	8	16	24	32	40	48	56	64	72	80	88	96
4×4	2 2/3	5 1/3	8	10 2/3	13 1/3	16	18 2/3	21 1/3	24	26 2/3	29 1/3	32
4×6	4	8	12	16	20	24	28	32	36	40	44	48
4×8	5 1/3	10 2/3	16	21 1/3	26 2/3	32	37 1/3	42 2/3	48	53 1/3	58 2/3	64
4×10	6 2/3	13 1/3	20	26 2/3	33 1/3	40	46 2/3	53 1/3	60	66 2/3	73 1/3	80
4×12	8	16	24	32	40	48	56	64	72	80	88	96
4×14	9 1/3	18 2/3	28	37 1/3	46 2/3	56	65 1/3	74 2/3	84	93 1/3	102 2/3	112
4×16	10 2/3	21 1/3	32	42 2/3	53 1/3	64	74 2/3	85 1/3	96	106 2/3	117 1/3	128
6×6	6	12	18	24	30	36	42	48	54	60	66	72
6×8	8	16	24	32	40	48	56	64	72	80	88	96
6×10	10	20	30	40	50	60	70	80	90	100	110	120
6×12	12	24	36	48	60	72	84	96	108	120	132	144
6×14	14	28	42	56	70	84	98	112	126	140	154	168
6×16	16	32	48	64	80	96	112	128	144	160	176	192
6×18	18	36	54	72	90	108	126	144	162	180	198	216
6×20	20	40	60	80	100	120	140	160	180	200	220	240
6×22	22	44	66	88	110	132	154	176	198	220	242	264
6×24	24	48	72	96	120	144	168	192	216	240	264	288
8×8	10 2/3	21 1/3	32	42 2/3	53 1/3	64	74 2/3	85 1/3	96	106 2/3	117 1/3	128
8×10	13 1/3	26 2/3	40	53 1/3	66 2/3	80	93 1/3	106 2/3	120	133 1/3	146 2/3	160
8×12	16	32	48	64	80	96	112	128	144	160	176	192
8×14	18 2/3	37 1/3	56	74 2/3	93 1/3	112	130 2/3	149 1/3	168	186 2/3	205 1/3	224
8×16	21 1/3	42 2/3	64	85 1/3	106 2/3	128	149 1/3	170 2/3	192	213 1/3	234 2/3	256
8×18	24	48	72	96	120	144	168	192	216	240	264	288
8×20	26 2/3	53 1/3	80	106 2/3	133 1/3	160	186 2/3	213 1/3	240	266 2/3	293 1/3	320
8×22	29 1/3	58 2/3	88	117 1/3	146 2/3	176	205 1/3	234 2/3	264	293 1/3	322 2/3	352
8×24	32	64	96	128	160	192	224	256	288	320	352	384
10×10	16 2/3	33 1/3	50	66 2/3	83 1/3	100	116 2/3	133 1/3	150	166 2/3	183 1/3	200
10×12	20	40	60	80	100	120	140	160	180	200	220	240
10×14	23 1/3	46 2/3	70	93 1/3	116 2/3	140	163 1/3	186 2/3	210	233 1/3	256 2/3	280
10×16	26 2/3	53 1/3	80	106 2/3	133 1/3	160	186 2/3	213 1/3	240	266 2/3	293 1/3	320
10×18	30	60	90	120	150	180	210	240	270	300	330	360
10×20	33 1/3	66 2/3	100	133 1/3	166 2/3	200	233 1/3	266 2/3	300	333 1/3	366 2/3	400
10×22	36 2/3	73 1/3	110	146 2/3	183 1/3	220	256 2/3	293 1/3	330	366 2/3	403 1/3	440
10×24	40	80	120	160	200	240	280	320	360	400	440	480

ELECTRICAL USAGE OF COMMON APPLIANCES

Electric Appliance	Average Wattage	Estimated Average kWH Monthly	Average Operating Cost/Mo. @ 4¢ kWH
Bed Covering	175	30	$ 1.20
Broiler	1,435	9	.36
Clock	2	1 1/2	.06
Coffee Maker	895	8	.32
Deep Fat Fryer	1,450	7	.28
Dishwasher	1,200	30	1.20
Fan (Circulating)	85	12	.48
Food Mixer	125	1	.04
Food Waste Disposer	440	3	.12
Frying Pan	1,200	16	.64
Hair Dryer	380	1 1/2	.06
Oven, Microwave (only)	1,450	19	.76
Radio	70	7	.28
Radio - Record Player	100	10	.40
Range and Oven	12,200	100	4.00
Range and Oven (Self Cleaning)	12,200	105	4.20
Refrigerator, 12 cu.ft. Non-Frostless	240	60	2.40
Refrigerator, 12 cu.ft. Frostless	320	102	4.08
Refrigerator-Freezer			
14 cu.ft. Non-Frostless	475	140	5.60
14 cu.ft. Frostless	610	160	6.40
18 cu.ft. Frostless	720	190	7.60
21 cu.ft. Frostless	750	218	8.72
Roaster	1,345	20	.80
Sewing Machine	75	1	.04
Television, B & W, Tube	200	35	1.40
Television, B & W, Solid State	55	10	.40
Television, Color, Tube	330	55	2.20
Television, Color, Solid State	200	35	1.40

Sources

For more information on some of the products and services available to help you remodel your attic, basement or garage, write to the following:

AMERICAN PLYWOOD ASSOCIATION
(Building materials)
P.O. Box 11700
Tacoma, WA 98411

AMERICAN HOME LIGHTING INSTITUTE
(Lighting information)
435 N. Michigan Ave.
Chicago, IL 60611-4067

AMERICAN STANDARD
(Kitchen and bathroom fixtures)
3 Crossroads of Commerce
Suite 100
Rolling Meadows, IL 60008

ANDERSEN CORPORATION
(Windows and skylights)
Bayport, MN 55003

CELOTEX CORPORATION
(Building materials)
P.O. Box 22602
Tampa, FL 33622

DOW CHEMICAL COMPANY
(Building materials)
2020 Dow Center
Midland, MI 48640

GEORGIA-PACIFIC CORPORATION
(Building materials)
133 Peachtree Street, NE
P.O. Box 105605
Atlanta, GA 30348-4000

KOHLER COMPANY
(Bathroom and kitchen fixtures)
Kohler, WI 53044

LOUISIANA-PACIFIC CORPORATION
(Building materials)
111 SW Fifth Avenue
Portland, OR 97204

NUTONE PRODUCTS
(Heaters, fans, bathroom accessories)
Madison & Red Bank Roads
Cincinnati, OH 45227

SPECTRUM CONSTRUCTION
(Remodeling services)
P.O. Box 968
Bend, OR 97709

VELUX-AMERICA CORPORATION
(Skylights)
450 Old Brickyard Rd.
P.O. Box 3208
Greenwood, SC 29648

WESTERN WOOD PRODUCTS ASSOCIATION
(Building materials)
522 SW Fifth Avenue
Portland, OR 97204-2122

WILSONART LAMINATES
(Plastic laminates)
600 General Bruce Dr.
Temple, TX 76501

WOOD MOULDING AND MILLWORK
   Producers Association
(Molding information)
P.O. Box 25278
Portland, OR 97225

Index

Other Bestsellers of Related Interest

INCREASE ITS WORTH: 101 Ways To Maximize The Value of Your Home—Jonathan Erickson

"...an idea book, filled with sensible advice on what makes a home valuable."—**San Francisco Examiner**

The author profiles the three basic types of home buyers, defines the factors that affect resale value, explains two basic methods of determining your home's resale value, and shows you what rooms play the biggest role in deciding the value of a home. 208 pages, 105 illustrations. Book No. 3073, $14.95 paperback, $23.95 hardcover

KITCHEN REMODELING—A Do-It-Yourselfer's Guide—Paul Bianchina

"...offers all the know-how you need to remodel a kitchen economically and attractively."—**Country Accents**

Create a kitchen that meets the demands of your lifestyle. With this guide you can attractively and economically remodel your kitchen yourself. All the know-how you need is supplied in this complete step-by-step reference, from planning and measuring to installation and finishing. 206 pages, 187 illustrations. Book No. 3011, $14.95 paperback, $23.95 hardcover

FENCES, DECKS AND OTHER BACKYARD PROJECTS—2nd Edition—Dan Ramsey

Do-it-yourself—design, build, and landscape fences and other outdoor structures. The most complete guide available for choosing, installing, and properly maintaining every kind of fence imaginable. Plus, there are how-tos for a variety of outdoor structures, from sheds and decks to greenhouses and gazebos. Easy-to-follow instructions, work-in-progress diagrams, tables, and hundreds of illustrations. 304 pages, Illustrated. Book No. 2778, $14.95 paperback, $22.95 hardcover

WHOLE HOUSE REMODELING GUIDE—S. Blackwell Duncan

This book features hundreds of remodeling, renovating, and redecorating options described and illustrated step-by-step! Focusing on interior modeling, the possibilities that exist for floors, windows, doors, walls, and ceilings are comprehensively explored. Complete detailed, illustrated instructions for projects are easy to follow. 448 pages, Illustrated. Book No. 3281, $16.95 paperback, $24.95 hardcover

KITCHEN AND BATHROOM CABINETS—Percy W. Blandford

Kitchen and Bathroom Cabinets is a collection of wooden cabinet projects that will help you organize and modernize your kitchen and bathroom and make them more attractive at the same time. Clear step-by-step instructions and detailed drawings enable you to build wall and floor cabinets and counters, corner cupboards, island units, built-in tables, worktables, breakfast bars, vanities, and more. 300 pages, 195 illustrations. Book No. 3244, $16.95 paperback, $26.95 hardcover

WHAT'S IT WORTH: A Home Inspection and Appraisal Manual—Joseph V. Scaduto

"...replete with diagrams and written in language that can be understood by even the most novice house seeker...a must for anyone looking at older houses."—**The Boston Globe**

"...a truly no-nonsense manual for home buyers to use in a self-inspection process."—**New York Public Library, New Technical Books**

This book is packed with practical advice that could save you hundreds, even thousands of dollars in unexpected home maintenance and repair costs! 288 pages, 299 illustrations. Book No. 3301, $16.95 paperback, $24.95 hardcover

BASIC BLUEPRINTING READING—John A. Nelson

With the knowledge gained from this book, you will become expert at reading not only mechanical drawings, but construction, electrical, and plumbing drawings as well. Using a step-by-step approach, John Nelson incorporates the latest ANSI drafting standards as he covers all aspects of blueprint reading. Through straightforward language and excellent example illustrations, Nelson shows you how to identify and understand one-view, multi-view, sectional-view, and auxiliary-view drawings. 256 pages, 235 illustrations. Book No. 3273, $18.95 paperback, $27.95 hardcover

Other Bestsellers of Related Interest

GARAGES: Complete Step-by-Step Building Plans— Ernie Bryant

A tremendous savings if you elect to contract out the project are the five building plans included in this book for garages in cape, colonial, and contemporary styles. One-, two-, and three-car garages, with or without living quarters above, are featured. These plans used with Bryant's explicit, illustrated, step-by-step instructions make it possible for you to build an attractive garage without the added cost of hiring professional help. 192 paperback, 127 illustrations. Book No. 3314, $14.95 paperback, $22.95 hardcover

MAKE YOUR HOUSE RADON FREE—Drs. Carl and Barbara Giles

Safeguard your home and family from the dangers of radon using this practical guide. What radon is, what it does, how it enters your home or workplace, how to remove it, and how to prevent it from recurring are covered in detail. Specific brands of radon-measuring and radon-deterring equipment, products, and materials are recommended. Tips on building a radon resistant home are also included. 144 pages, Illustrated. Book No. 3291, $9.95 paperback, $15.95 hardcover

Look for These and Other TAB Books at Your Local BOOKSTORE

To Order Call Toll Free 1-800-822-8158
(in PA and AK call 717-794-2191)

or write to TAB BOOKS Inc., Blue Ridge Summit, PA 17294-0840.

Title	Product No.	Quantity	Price

☐ Check or money order made payable to TAB BOOKS Inc.

Charge my ☐ VISA ☐ MasterCard ☐ American Express

Acct. No. _____ Exp. _____

Signature: _____

Name: _____

City: _____

State: _____ Zip: _____

Subtotal $	_____
Postage and Handling ($3.00 in U.S., $5.00 outside U.S.) $	_____
In PA, NY, & ME add applicable sales tax $	_____
TOTAL $	_____

TAB BOOKS catalog free with purchase; otherwise send $1.00 in check or money order and receive $1.00 credit on your next purchase.

Orders outside U.S. must pay with international money order in U.S. dollars.

TAB Guarantee: If for any reason you are not satisfied with the book(s) you order, simply return it (them) within 15 days and receive a full refund. **BC**